School Management and Multi-Professional Partnerships

Also available from Continuum

School Management and Multi-Professional Partnerships

Edited by
Raymond Moorcroft and Geoff Caton

continuum

Continuum International Publishing Group

The Tower Building   80 Maiden Lane
11 York Road   Suite 704
London SE1 7NX   New York NY 10038

www.continuumbooks.com

British Library Cataloguing-in-Publication Data
A catalogue record for this book is available from the British Library.

ISBN: 9780826494658 (hardcover)

Library of Congress Cataloging-in-Publication Data
A catalog record for this book is available from the Library of Congress.

Typeset by Newgen Imaging Systems Pvt Ltd, Chennai, India
Printed and bound in Great Britain by the MPG Books Group

Contents

List of Contributors

Val Butcher, Senior Lecturer, Institute of Education, Manchester Metropolitan University

Geoff Caton, Operational Director, Centre for Innovation and Enterprise, Manchester Metropolitan University

Mat Chapman, Skills for Life Manager, First UK Bus

Joy Coulbeck, MA Course Leader, Centre for Innovation and Enterprise, Manchester Metropolitan University

Angela Harnett, Programme Manager, Manchester Metropolitan University

Graham Lewis, Chief Executive, Everton in the Community

Ron Lofkin, Principal School Adviser, Secondary, Stockport MBC

Paul Matthews, Managing Director, Business for Education, Ltd.

Dr. Jonathan Middleton, Principal Educational Psychologist, St. Helens MBC

Ray Moorcroft, Director, Centre for Innovation and Enterprise, Manchester Metropolitan University

Inspector Saied Mostaghel, Merseyside Police

Bob Rawlinson, Chief Executive, The de Bono Foundation, UK

Nick Wrigley, former Secondary Headteacher; Senior Assessor, Certificate in School Business Management

Tim Yates, General Manager, NCSL Learning and Conference Center

Introduction: New Leaders . . . New Relationships

The management and leadership role in schools is increasingly spread over a number of people in the institution, and a number of new roles are emerging. For example, the School Business Manager (SBM) is now recognized as an integral part of a school structure, and according to the latest NCSL research (NCSL, 2007), over 70 per cent of those completing the Diploma in School Business Management (DSBM) are members of the senior management/leadership team. Some people call this 'distributed leadership' (Davies, Harris, *et al.*, 1990) but this implies a limited amount of leadership in the school. This book is about more than 'spreading' leadership – it is about innovation in managing and leading relationships, which we would argue has an unlimited potential . . . but more of this later.

Whether these structural changes are part of the cause or the reaction is not clear, but nationally and internationally, schools are evolving to become institutions which are better regarded as extended and community centres of learning. This means that, in addition to managing internal staff, headteachers and members of school leadership and management teams will increasingly encounter other staff and professionals who work with and within schools. This evolution is not yet complete, so the word 'school' will be used throughout this book, but it should be stressed that there is an implicit wider meaning attached. When we say 'school', we mean a centre of learning (hence the label, 'learning centre' used in some chapters) which has health services, probation, social services, community involvement, financial and transport infrastructures focused around it. Similarly, we use the term 'School Business Team' (SBT), because this book focuses on the professionals who interact and influence the 'business' of the school.

So who *are* these 'other staff and professionals'? Well, the list is not exclusive, but the activity areas in this book which have been selected are those which impact most on the school – whether currently or potentially – and where there is a 'new' relationship. Some of these relationships may not even be established yet . . . but they will have to be, sooner or later. The book is organized into three Parts. The first part relates to the concept of human beings as 'resources', and therefore focuses on generic information and advice about building and monitoring relationships with others who are 'professionals' in their own right. To help bring some structure to the range of relationships the book is organized into two further parts, reflecting the two broad divisions of human resources involved. The 'internal' staff are those who are directly involved in schools, although not necessarily on a daily basis. The 'external' personnel are those who have more indirect, but no less influential, contact with schools and the internal staff. Both sets have personnel new to schools and some who have worked for some time in schools, but whose role is changing. The warning note here is that one is not more important than the other.

New ways for old . . .

Globally, governments provide no job descriptions, organization structures or model processes for these new relationships, arguing that every school is unique and different. This new context therefore demands alternative and innovative strategies to develop new working relationships. The book provides examples of such strategies written by and based on the experiences of these other professionals, and through these case studies builds up a framework for action for Senior Leadership Teams (SLTs). In this book we would argue that the term 'SLT' is not always appropriate in this area of activity, and will therefore occasionally use the term, 'School Business Team' (SBT), as more appropriate in the context of schools as 'businesses'. Cameron Dugmore, the Minister for Education in Western Cape, South Africa, prefers to note that 'although a school is not a business, it should be run as a business'.

This quasi-business context is, of course, a far cry from the situation where the school came under the direct control of an 'Authority' or a 'District', and the staff in turn were directed by the headteacher in a strictly hierarchical relationship. The complexity of these new relationships is increased because of the interlocking nature of the services involved – and it has to be acknowledged that this is a positive development. It is also something which reflects the five principles of the UK's key education policy, 'Every Child Matters'.

- be safe
- be healthy
- enjoy and achieve
- make a positive contribution
- achieve economic well-being

Which in turn is reflected internationally in, for example, the USA, where the catchphrase is: 'No Child Left Behind'.

The complexity of these new agendas can be seen in a single example: that of school transport. This is currently the responsibility of local authorities/ districts, although some federated schools have considered separate arrangements. Further, if one-off school trips are involved, then it is generally the responsibility of the particular school. Dealing with transport managers is not something most school staff have been trained to do, and there can be a tendency to either 'trust the professionals' or to attempt to apply internal control approaches and systems to these external agencies. For example, at a simple level, the issue of child protection may cause some tensions, as the school manager may demand more from the bus company than is reasonable or financially viable. These demands may help the school comply with its own internal practices, but may be based on, for example, the framework which applies to temporary teaching staff, which in turn may not be appropriate for other roles. In practice, the situation demands a discrete approach to maximize the effectiveness of the relationship.

There is also a changed *legal context* applied to each of these situations, with the twin pressures of schools having to take more responsibility for their actions, and the increasingly litigious nature of society. These pressures are reflected in this book, with the overall perspective being that of mutuality of legal liability. In other words, both parties are culpable, unless one party is negligent. In this case negligence can be defined as non-compliance with any relevant law, but more normally and practically, with stated policies and procedural systems. The book adopts a 'light touch' with regard to legal guidance, and the disclaimers at the front are 'normal' in publications, but nevertheless offer sensible advice . . . basically, no one contributor can be held liable for a reader acting on the advice. However, we would contend that the sections in this book represent the most authoritative guidance available on a wide range of activities relevant to schools. They are selected as being of specific interest and provide current, practical and pragmatic advice for creating a safe and successful school.

The good, not the bad (or ugly!)

Perhaps more importantly, the book takes a positive view, focusing on exemplars of good practice, rather than giving a series of 'Don't . . .' warnings. It is up to each reader to pick up the transferable elements of good practice and apply/interpret them to her or his own situation. This in itself raises the interesting issue of 'transferability' of not just practice activity, but also of the underlying concepts and themes. There is a persistent view that, for schools, there is nothing to be learned from industrial and commercial fields of activity. This view has less credibility in the twenty-first century and in the UK, the National College for School Leadership (NCSL) has done much to help dispel the notion, as have educational management pioneer authors such as John West-Burnham, Brent Davies and Linda Ellison (Davies *et al.*, 1990), but it is still stubbornly evident in most schools. However, the external context will probably have more influence in eradicating the perspective than any such literature. The catalysts are:

1. The increasing acceptance of foundation-status schools, as the local authorities lose critical mass in terms of capability of support services.
2. The very nature of leadership and management thinking and its current manifestation in 'distributed leadership'.

To educationalists, the first catalyst is rooted in the Education Reform Acts of 1986 and 1988, but it could also be said to originate from 'futures thinking' by Western governments of that time, which argued that 'knowledge capital' and discrete, niche skills of individuals were the basis of future prosperity. Indeed, Margaret Thatcher famously stated that 'there was no such thing as society'. The present government's emphasis on personalized learning is arguably a logical extension of this approach. It was therefore a short step to move to local provision to suit individual needs and structurally, the introduction of a type of school which has its independence (of local authority control) as a 'foundation', is appropriate for a changed context. In practical terms, the option of 'buying in' services has led to an emasculation of many branches of the local authority services as schools have explored other avenues – usually commercial enterprises – which they deem more effective. Many schools have even established in-house replacement services (refer to the case study below) with attendant financial benefits. The similarity to industrial/commercial contexts is overwhelming, and therefore the 'external' view holds credibility, with many of the contributors in that section noting the efficiency savings of such approaches.

Case study: School catering

The school has been with the LEA catering service forever, and I have investigated fully contracting out to one of the big companies such as Sodexho or Scorest, but this was simply too risky to commit to the long term within the context of falling numbers.

So I am recommending to our governors that we take our catering in-house, supported by a company called Foodservice Options. This is a specialist organization providing a range of services to schools which self-manage their catering operation. They negotiate prices with suppliers which form the basis of the contract and the suppliers pay Foodservice Options a commission. Schools can then use the recommended suppliers as they have been through a tender process focusing on best value on a regular basis.

There are three options of service level agreement, with different levels of service offered for each: the 'gold' option is recommended for the first year as it's a transition period. The company advises on menus, provides nutritional guidance (including supplying the nutritional content on the menu in 2009, undertakes audits to ensure we meet legal requirements, offers training and so on.

I estimate our savings will be £13,500+, but we will have additional costs of approximately £2,200, leaving net gain of approximately £11,000.

The new service will be launched with a competition for the children to choose a new name for the canteen.

The second catalyst which will move schools to a more widespread acceptance of industrial/commercial concepts is the very nature of leading-edge thinking about leadership and management. The concept of 'distributed leadership' is very much the focus of NCSL research and thinking (NCSL, 2004/2006) with programmes entitled 'Leading from the Middle' exemplifying the approach. This has been reinforced by the PricewaterhouseCoopers study, 2007, (PwC, 2007) which overtly describes and recommends an extended role for the 'business manager'. Again, the definition and approach are based on industrial/commercial research and operational contexts and represent a more complex model. The approach is based on the phrase, 'leadership at all levels', first used by Peter Wickens in 1995. Other research, both earlier (Stodgill in 1974, Handy in 1991) and later (Drath, 1998) reaffirms the interest in the concept.

Oh, by the way, it is also important to distinguish between 'leadership at all levels' and that of 'distributed leadership': although the two may be grouped together there is a difference in implication. 'Distributed leadership' implies that there is a set amount of 'leadership' and this is 'distributed' throughout the organization by the head. 'Leadership at all levels' is a more organic approach which implies that there is no limit to the 'store of leadership', rather, each level negotiates a 'seed' which is then nurtured by the leader at that level. The results may not be a tidy organizational shape, but the approach *does* encourage synergy. With regard to learning centres, I believe the concept of 'leadership at all levels' is more appropriate.

In any event, the key point is that:

> Although [much literature] suggests that leadership exists only at the very top, leaders in fact, achieve results by working with and through people, and [leadership] can and should be present at all levels of the organization.
>
> Although the top leader is often vital to the success of the organization, can set its tone and sometimes transform its values, such leaders, working alone, achieve nothing.
>
> (Wickens, 1995)

In the case of schools, heads have long accepted that there's too much for any one person to do, so again, there is an obvious element of transference. So, if we accept that we *can* learn from non-education-based contexts, then the examples of good practice should be pored over to see what you, as a reader can get from them . . . I guarantee there'll be something for every reader!

The bad . . . but still not ugly . . .!

Nevertheless, it would be naïve to accept that there are no problems with dealing with 'other' professionals. The example of transport given above highlights some potential problems, and that is exactly what each chapter goes on to examine. Each contributor has been asked to identify the key issues in their particular area of activity: they may not be 'show-stoppers' in themselves, but may in the longer term combine to produce a real problem. It's noticeable that most revolve around relationships and inter-personal transactions rather than say, resources, but this in itself reflects organizational studies and people's instinctive feelings about working life. Indeed, the old saying that 'school would be a great place without the children' could be amended to . . . 'school would be a great place without the staff!'

Again, the approach adopted is for you, the reader, to examine these issues and reflect on their applicability to your situation/context. The key point to remember, and the value of these 'lists' of issues is that they represent the views of the people concerned as *they* perceive the role. You may not agree, or think that a particular issue applies to you, but their perceptions are your reality. In other words, you can't work to your own terms of reference, but you have to work to others' terms of reference . . . unless you decide to go down the route of attempting to *change* others' views, beliefs and values. The problems attached to this course of action will probably be greater than simply responding to the reality of others! As Mikhail Gorbachev noted, 'The human spirit does not easily adapt to change.'

So what you have here are issues which demand action from you in order to solve or mitigate them. Take a look at the example in the box below.

If a school has received a number of complaints from both residents and parents about cooking smells/fumes coming from the kitchen, and health and safety officials recommend that the extraction system and filters need upgrading, then the catering company may face a dilemma. Their actions will almost certainly be guided by industrial/commercial/legal considerations – not least that of finance and profitability – and commercial companies generally abide by the legal principle of Best Available Technique Not Entailing Excessive Cost (BATNEEC). A mouthful, but in reality, this is a principle which prevents companies from becoming bankrupt because they have to implement legislation in every respect. In this case, if the company can show that (say) installing an enhanced extraction system would be prohibitively expensive, with no hope of recovering expenditure, then putting in (say) an extra window would be acceptable. The school business team may have to review the school's policies, undertake a risk assessment covering, for example, the extent of time the children are exposed to the fumes, balancing that factor with the complaints from local residents and then agree a way forward with the company.

In this case, the school has to do the work and still not get what it really wants. It sounds a little one-sided and unfair, doesn't it? However, there is help in this book!

The assistance is provided through the case studies and the 'breaks'.

Help . . .??

In the activities and case studies, we ask you to continually apply principle to practice – but don't worry, we don't expect you to do it on your own. This is where you look at what each contributor has provided, that is, a description of the terms of reference for the particular role/area of activity they are involved in. The specific behaviours and actions which the particular role demands are set out so that each party involved in the relationship can have clear expectations of the other. This is not a 'wish list', but a realistic summary of the behaviours that school management can ask for from the person undertaking the role. The legal context for these behaviours is that of 'the man on the Clapham omnibus': in other words, would this be regarded by the 'man in the street' as a reasonable request. For example, it would not be unreasonable to insist on a dress code for contractors working in the school, and to have a right to veto where necessary. This will be increasingly important in the context of the new 14–19 curriculum where 'trades education' will be the norm, and taught best practice could be undermined by inappropriate clothes which may even have health and safety implications if copied. It would also be 'reasonable' to expect certain standards of civility in the exchanges which may be necessary to ensure the agreement is enforced!

So now you have the theory and the expectations for a satisfactory standard of interaction with your 'other' professionals . . . but it's only a start. What this book is really about is taking the relationships and activities involved to a new level of quality. It's too presumptuous to say that each activity area will become 'excellent' if you follow the advice contained here, but there is an imperative in that it has to be aspirational . . . being better than it was and certainly beyond satisfactory. The key is to ensure that there are strategies and systems in place which will ensure there is an emphasis on improvement. You can do this in a formal manner through externally accredited systems such as ISO 9001, or set up internal programmes and documentation which focus on continuous quality improvement (CQI). Strangely, the latter approach is most favoured by school leaders and managers who perceive the formal quality systems to be too onerous, but in fact the reverse is true. The internal and external audits which are a necessary part of, for example, ISO 9001 gradually become so much a part of everyday working practices that improvement is almost inevitable and the system itself prevents 'fall-back'.

Interestingly, over 90 per cent of UK companies now have this standard and it is regarded as a condition of being accepted as a supplier by most large companies and by the DCSF.

Fit for what purpose?

The DTI defines quality in the ISO sense as: 'Fitness for Purpose and safe in use. It is the service provided or product designed and constructed to satisfy the customers' needs'.

Put more pragmatically, what we're talking about here is a management system which indicates HOW quality is provided and guaranteed by the organization. Nobody says the system has to produce perfect goods or services, but the system guarantees that, whatever the circumstances, the outcome will be what the organization says it should be. It's a framework of procedures which the organization must use to achieve the quality which the organization says it will provide. Obviously some people argue that therefore the system can be excellent and the organization can produce poor quality services, provided it does so consistently – absolutely correct! However, this argument ignores the fact that the organization wouldn't stay in business very long if that was the case . . . The easiest and longer-term way of looking at it is as a system which enables a company to introduce Total Quality Management (TQM), because it sets a benchmark which must be 'bettered' every year.

Contrast this to an approach which demands much of its leadership and management team in terms of constantly reiterating the need to do things better, and then having to monitor, evaluate and review several different data sets, collected through several different channels and processes. Benchmarking is not an easy option in that particular scenario!

In the case of 'managing the professionals', there is another advantage in the more formal approach. The emphasis on quality through a more formal system will be particularly welcomed by the external organizations and personnel who are familiar with (particularly) ISO 9001. Over 97 per cent of UK organizations are now registered with one of the five main accrediting bodies and therefore almost every employee, *and parent*, will recognize the approach. In turn, of course, this makes the emphasis on quality improvement even more an integral part of working relationships. Therefore each chapter also focuses on strategies which school managers can adopt to maximize the usefulness of the particular role in question. Remember also that, in effect, you are managing without power when you manage 'other staff and professionals – there is no real control in terms of employment law. So each chapter focuses on a practical and pragmatic approach, but one which again, demands managers use their skills to analyse these strategies and make a coherent strategy for *their* school . . . because every school is different, and will be different in the future. The key to future success as a learning centre is to make sure that the creativity, flexibility and responsiveness which others possess is used to enhance the core purpose of the organization. What the core purpose is . . . well, you know what that is for your organization . . . and if you don't, then close this book now and sort that out first!

References and further reading

Davies, B., Ellison, L., Osborne A. and West-Burnham J. (1990), *Education Management for the 1990s*. London: Longman.

Drath, W. H. (1998), 'Approaching the future of leadership development', in C. D. McCauley, R. S. Moxley and E. Van Velsor (eds), *Handbook of Leadership Development*. San Francisco: Jossey-Bass, pp. 403–32.

Handy, C. B. (1991), *Understanding Organizations*. London: Penguin Books Ltd.

NCSL (2007), *Impact and Evaluation* report.

NCSL publications and programmes (2004), *Tidying the Cupboard? The Role of Subject Leaders in Primary Schools*.

NCSL publications and programmes (2006), *Rethinking Leadership Roles in Secondary Schools*.

PwC (2007), *Independent Study into School Leadership: Main Report*. London: DfES.

Stodgill, R. M. (1974), *Handbook of Leadership: A Survey of Theory and Research*. New York: The Free Press.

Wickens, P. (1995), *The Ascendant Organization*. Basingstoke: Palgrave Macmillan.

Part One
Managing Relationships

Establishing Relationships

Ray Moorcroft and Geoff Caton

1

Chapter Outline

1.1 Introduction

Man is primarily a social organism. People need people, with social interaction a feature of daily life – unless you're a self-sufficient hermit! This chapter focuses on the types of relationship which exist in the interactions between the professionals who are involved in educating children. It will examine the factors that influence the building and maintenance of these relationships in any sector activity, but will also apply these variables to the specific and discrete context of the education sector.

The move to a market-led approach of education provision by successive UK governments is a trend which has been closely observed and tentatively followed by other countries. The growing presence and awareness of these 'other' professionals in schools illustrates the effect of these radical changes in the way educational institutions are now organized, with 'outsourcing' a relatively common phenomenon. This means that the suppositions which have existed regarding the 'management' of such service providers have been made obsolete by changes in the relationship. Nevertheless, many schools persist in following the 'old', traditional ways of interacting with their fellow professionals, and thus miss out on the potential to use creative approaches to get the best out of them. One useful analogy may be to think of these 'other professionals' in the way that business thinks about 'relationship marketing' as a strategy for successfully working with its customers. The challenge of this chapter is therefore to arouse your creativity and explore innovation with regard to maximizing the resource on offer – but perhaps the biggest challenge is to devise a set of criteria which will enable you to know your innovative approach has paid off . . . or not! If it doesn't (and it's not your fault), well, you'll also be shown how to 'complain and sustain' so that the service can be enhanced!

1.2 Social interaction: Building the relationship

Man is primarily a social organism, so we use this term ('social interaction'), rather than 'professional interaction' for two reasons: first, because it signifies that most of the issues we encounter are generic. The greatest pleasures and the greatest distress are experienced at the hands of others – and this applies to both work and play. The other reason is that it can be readily identified as a distinct discipline (social psychology) being a rich field for psychologists, with resultant in-depth research to back up the key points.

Social interaction takes place whenever one person's behaviour is significantly affected by the presence or behaviour of another person. Social psychology focuses on the individual in relation to other individuals (the implications and influences on the relationship), rather than on the individual in isolation (which is 'psychology'). The effects of other individuals on the relationship range from the effect of somebody merely being present, to the influence of those we regard as peers. This latter interaction is where we would wish to focus, but it's worth noting that here, the influences are subtle and indirect, and operate at many levels. For example, a discussion with an educational psychologist (a 'peer professional') may provide new information, may develop or may inhibit our thinking about other people/students, or simply reinforce an existing antipathy we hold towards 'ed. psychs'.

In any event, there are a number of variables to consider in building up a relationship with our peers, each of which will be considered in turn:

- the presence of others
- individual and group motivation
- social roles
- conformity culture
- communications

1.3 Presence

There are basically two levels of presence: 'being there' and (inter) active. Merely 'being there' inevitably influences the situation to some degree – ask any parent about the 'audience effect' on children's behaviour! Imagine then, the consequences to your own behaviour of someone whom you respect/dislike simply being at the same meeting. People interpret the other's presence in different ways: 'oh, they always disagree with me, so I'll say nothing' or 'goodness, she's so well known, she's bound to be right, so I'll say nothing'! In the Peter Sellers's film of the same title, simply 'being there' produced all sorts of misinterpretations, with hilarious effects, while in research, the issue of interaction between subject(s) and researcher (where the effect is considerably heightened), is studied as ethnography.

This phenomenon is complicated by the small matter of person perception, where variables such as verbal labels have a great influence on the process of forming impressions of people – particularly important when there has been little actual interaction or observation of the individual.

Take a look at the activity set out in the box below:

Take a break . . . First impressions

What is your impression of this person? This individual has been described as . . . energetic, assured, talkative, cold, ironical, inquisitive, persuasive.
   Please write your own descriptive evaluation of him.

This exercise was based on a famous experiment in 1946 by Asch when more than 1,000 college students were asked, 'what is your impression of this person?'

The results were remarkable: the students gave complete personal descriptions, adding other features and traits to the profile – I'm sure you didn't do this!

However, more significantly for our purposes, there were distinct behavioural differences when, in a follow-up experiment in 1950 by Kelley, the description was modified. When introducing a facilitator, the sentence, 'People who know him consider him to be a rather cold person, industrious, critical, practical and determined' was given to one half of an audience, and ONE WORD was changed in the sentence given to the other half. That word was 'warm'. The half judging the 'warm' person participated in discussions much more freely, and rated the person more favourably than those judging the 'cold' person. Obviously, perceptions of the person influenced behaviour.

So, what can we do about this? Well actually, you've already done something. By reading this far, you are now aware of the powerful influence *anyone* can have on an interaction – right from first impressions. You will also now be aware of the danger of regarding someone favourably because they share (say) the same social values or likes, or even because you 'know them' (even though you've only met them twice before!), whereas you don't know anyone else in the meeting. This phenomenon is actually true: experiments which involved people looking at photographs of perfect strangers (Zajonc, 1968), illustrate that people express a greater liking for those whose photographs they've seen more often!

Therefore accept that there *is* an effect, rather than believe that you will 'behave exactly the same with everyone' and that this raised awareness is the most positive response. It's a bit like 'weight watchers': the concept works on the basis that people have to say out loud their target, and this simple action is reckoned to enhance the chances of slimming success. Therefore actually saying in the first meeting that there may be certain preconceptions which may influence the relationship will enhance the chances of success in terms of minimizing a skewed relationship. This doesn't have to be confrontational: something like, 'Look, I've not had much to do with you, but people tell me you have certain views and methods: can we spend a few minutes just setting out what is important to us in this area of activity?' will do the trick.

By the way, it is a noticeable feature of several of the contributors' chapters that this initial meeting is regarded as essential to set the tone for the ongoing relationship.

1.4 Individual and group motivation

The Hay McBer group have undertaken research for the National College for School Leadership (NCSL, 2000) which informed the design of training programmes for prospective and existing leaders of schools. Their findings indicated that there were no substantial differences in the traits, qualities and motivation between those leaders operating in the educational sector, and those in the industrial/commercial world. The results were greeted with some media derision ('£4 million for stating the bl**ding obvious!'), but their value lay in the fact that programmes could be designed using that assumption of 'no difference'. This may be uncomfortable for those who take refuge in the phrase that 'schools are different', but for our purposes, the rationale works well in that we can establish common grounds for action, by assuming that what drives the professional service provider is what drives the educational professional.

Further, we can use the same model of motivation which allows us to regard individual motivation as consisting of three key elements: affiliation, achievement and power. The first (affiliation: the strong incentive value of one organism for another) is evident in both the animal and human worlds, but the other two seem to be uniquely human. Achievement has been the subject of an enormous amount of research (even into the achievement motive of nations!), but basically is about competition with self and others, and McLelland's work is worth looking at in this respect. Power is really the province of Alfred Adler who felt that power was even more important than sex as a motivator: it has several forms but basically involves wanting control of others, or a situation – for good or evil! These three elements account for 80 per cent of our behaviours in social interactions which is enough for us to use as a base for building relationships.

What does all this mean in practical terms? The following example (based on a real situation) will help illustrate the usefulness of the approach.

Take a break . . . Motivation

You have met with the builder on at least three occasions. The first phase (asking him what was important for him in building the extension to the toilets), was tricky . . . but eventually he got the idea. As an electrician, turned general builder, now running his own company, he had a conflict of values. He wanted to

---

Take a break—cont'd

ensure safety of the electrics at any cost, even to checking himself, but knew that there were budgets and other elements and sites that needed to be managed and overseen, which others regarded as equally important. He also recognized that, as a local authority project, he needed to be on time, and within budget, and had to work to a county project manager in order to preserve the chances of future business – someone whom he believed was not as qualified as himself. He also knew the pressures the school would face because, as a parent, he wanted this to be right, and knew the children would suffer if there were delays or problems.

From these 'critical conversations', it was clear that you, as the school manager, shared some of these concerns – not least the issue of perfection ('getting it right'). You recognize that the achievement motive is equally powerful in you both . . . a situation ripe for potential conflict, for who is to say what's 'right'?

How can you turn this to your advantage?

This knowledge (perhaps even shared) is invaluable in helping (both) professionals to avoid a confrontational start to the relationship, and to set terms of reference for future working. This can be done by agreeing the items/ activities that both regard as essential . . . and listing them! The trick is then to suppress the concerns regarding those elements which are not on the list, thus allowing 'achievement' for each partner.

So much for the motivation of the individual . . . what about the motivation of the group? Well, the first step is to recognize that there *is* such a thing as 'group motivation'. The second thing to acknowledge is that it can overwhelm individual motivation . . . the phenomena of mass hysteria, riots, public protests and so on, are evidence of the reality of both the existence of group motivation and of how it can be more powerful than the individual's will or sense of values.

In schools, group motivation is heightened by the relatively small numbers involved in each of the 'groups'. For example, the catering staff in a small primary school can quickly become united by some perceived slander about the food, and although individuals may be sceptical ('I don't believe she would say that'), the power of the rumour can overwhelm common sense. The desire (motivation) of the group to defend itself will be more powerful than the individual's affiliative motive.

Unfortunately, in this case, knowledge of theory is of less use: knowing that you share the perspectives of others is more agreeable than knowing it's wrong! What does this mean in practice? Let's go back to the builder . . . see box below.

Case study: The natives are getting restless

You and Alan (the builder) are getting along reasonably well, but you know that most of the staff (and especially the catering staff) don't like him: actually, they don't like builders in general because 'they don't care about anybody else, and we need to look after the children'.

Remember, you know this is not true because of your first meeting with Alan, so you ignore the complaints. However, one day, the water supply has to be cut off for an hour while the new mains supply is installed in the toilets. You've agreed the time, knowing that most of the children will be in lessons, and have made contingency arrangements for the 'emergencies'. Unfortunately, there is a problem, and the water is off for nearly two hours . . . just at the time the kitchen staff are preparing and serving food. Teaching staff have to help out with supervision, and it is touch-and-go about closing the school. The staff are furious, and are vociferous in their argument that this proves 'builders don't care' . . . they ask you to complain (over Alan's head) to the local authority engineer. Would YOU resist the demands?

The answer lies in prevention – making sure that communication channels are strong (and fast) enough to ensure the truth will (generally) emerge. Again, this requires a partnership approach with both parties talking to staff, *as the problem emerges*.

This may require some ingenuity, as it is obviously impossible to call a meeting every time such a problem occurs, but modern technology in schools does mean that video-conferencing and emails can be used as rapid-communication devices . . . and in the longer term, what's wrong with letting Alan host a brief 'hot seat'? Of course, the real and underlying issue here is that of social role.

1.5 Social role

This variable is probably one of the most powerful because it is deeply engrained within each individual. Much of our behaviour is influenced by the positions we hold in society, or perhaps more accurately, the perceived status of the positions we hold in 'our' society (the groups we belong to).

We all have perceptions about each of the roles we hold (mother, daughter, employee, secretary of a theatre group, and so on) and the expected behavioural obligations. Indeed, once we know these, we can reasonably predict the key features of a person's behaviour. The Leadership Programme for Serving heads (LPSH) programme operated (until 2007) by the National College for School Leadership (NCSL) alludes to the value of such knowledge in restraining/amending less acceptable behaviours in both self and others.

The problem in building relationships is the hierarchy of such roles. Let's have another look at the case study and the problem of the builder. It would be naïve to say that 'class' does not still exist in all societies. The caste system may have been castigated and weakened, but any visitor to Asia will see the evidence of its survival. The Western world enjoys some mobility between social classes, but increasingly, job-related (rather than birth-related) class is the norm. Just listen to any class of KS2 children for evidence of the phenomenon ('My dad's in computers'), and then consider your own perceptions of the hierarchy. Don't worry, it's 'normal' to have a mental hierarchy, but the social expectations attached to this situation are strong, and although they vary in different countries, the builder is 'below' the school staff in the social hierarchy, and should be 'put in their place'. It's that old Byzantine concept of 'class' which is rearing its head here. Unfortunately, this excessive social conformity can damage relationships.

1.6 Conformity culture

Let's stop and go back to basics here: schools are places for learning about living as much as gaining knowledge, and as such, are places which lean towards propounding social conformity as essential for living in any society. For example, abuse of fellow pupils or staff is a non-acceptable practice, and understanding that this can translate to problems in adult life is part of 'growing up'. However, unless it is coupled with an appreciation of what is 'right' (and 'wrong') for *both the individual and the group*, then it can lead to a conformity culture.

This balance of individual independent thought and conformity to social practice is a hard one to achieve and when out of balance can be distressing. When one thinks of the trials of War Criminals post-1945, and the standard reply of 'I was following orders', it is deeply disturbing to think of the effects of excessive social conformity. A recent example and a 'breather' is provided in the box below.

Take a break . . . Conformity

In 2002, the Nobel Prize for Economics went to a research psychologist who had never studied economics. Daniel Kahneman explored the concept of conformity in terms of stock market movements, observing that traders copied each other, leading to 'Bubbles and Booms'. How does this apply to education?

- Well let us give you an example: we will adapt a typical Kahneman experiment and ask you to think of the number of separate grains of sand in a typical handful . . . done it? It's 17,800.
- OK . . . now estimate the number of primary school teaching staff in London . . . done it?
- Now ask a number of colleagues to do the same.

Actually, the two sets of numbers have nothing to do with each other! However, Kahneman found that the correlation between the answers people gave was well beyond what might be expected by chance. The phenomenon is known as 'anchoring'.

He noted how we are all influenced by the numbers and 'facts' we are given, and we influenced you by telling you a (fictional) high number of grains of sand, and the chances are you will also err on the high side when you make your estimate of the number of teachers in the three cities.

PS: It's 26,000.

In schools, this culture can lead to lasting damage to children's self-esteem, as those pupils who don't conform are treated as 'geeks' or 'nerds'. Indeed, Hollywood loves this storyline for its 'teen movies' with 'Spider-Man' a recent example.

Psychologists haven't cracked this one yet, and reported cases of bullying in schools continue to rise inexorably. The only possible hope for an answer lies in the area of 'suggestibility', where imitation of behaviour seems to overwhelm the majority for a short time. The best example of this is yawning! We can be stimulated to imitate by simply seeing someone yawn – even on television. More practically, a case of sympathy for a victim may turn the tide of opinion in a school if that victim has simultaneous other problems (for example, a family bereavement). Unfortunately, the phenomenon doesn't seem to last long . . . it becomes a 'fad'. However, schools continue to make admirable efforts to change behaviours through modifying rules and 'modelling' – therefore the same principles can apply with reference to 'other professionals'. Why not have a set of protocols for staff in dealing with their 'external' colleagues? It doesn't have to be significantly different from that which applies to pupils. Of course, all the policies and protocols in the world won't make any difference to your relationship building unless both parties in the relationship understand fully what each is saying – or more accurately, what each is *trying* to say!

In other words, the key to effective relationship building is using all of the above knowledge to inform your approach to communications – understanding others' views and perceptions is the most effective way of changing attitudes and behaviours.

1.7 Persuasive communication

Let's keep this simple, there are three elements involved in 'persuasive communication' – the communicator, the message and the receiver. Remember your objective: to build a relationship with an 'external' professional. Therefore the starting point is yourself, as the 'communicator' and the key element is your credibility. There is overwhelming evidence that the more credible the communicator seems to be, the more effectively the message is communicated and the more readily the receiver accepts it. Although, even here, a famous experiment involving the poet T. S. Eliot showed that 'person perception' (liking/disliking someone on first sight) has an influence. However, let's assume a neutral perception in terms of your attraction (!) and continue. Your membership of the SLT gives you immediate credibility, but the extent of that credibility is limited to the receiver's *perception* of that status – i.e. what does this mean to others? To illustrate this, have a go at the activity in the box below.

Take a break . . . Benchmarking

Try this simple 'benchmarking' exercise: ask members of your social circle to 'rate' the *position* of a member of the SLT (not you as a person) in terms of status compared to, say, a company board member, a member of an NHS 'crash team', a quality inspection team (or Ofsted team member), and so on . . .

Any surprises?

Fortunately, awareness of social role, peer conformity, individual motivation and so on will inform your perception of your credibility, so obviously what you're doing here is checking the place in the social role hierarchy.

Now let's go back to Alan . . . what does *he* think of your role? Well it depends on how stereotypical you want to be. He *could* think very little of it ('So what? It means nothing in the real world.'), or he could give it even more status than you ('Wow. In charge of all these people.'). You could use the data collected from your benchmarking activity, but the key point is that you don't know for sure unless you find out from Alan . . . which brings us full circle back to the first meeting! In other words, it's up to you at that first meeting to ensure there are no misunderstandings or wrong perceptions. You have to get your message across.

Take a break . . . Creativity

Of course, in terms of impact of message, the more creative you are, the more the message gets home. Take a break . . . have a go at the task below.

In the late 1950s, Frank Barron came up with the idea of 'testing' for creativity. His experiment involved eight questions which are set out below. Grab yourself a sheet of paper and write true or false for each question – be honest with yourself!

Creative thinking

1. I like to fool around with new ideas, even if they turn out later to be a total waste of time.
2. The best theory is one that has the best practical application.
3. Some of my friends think that my ideas are impractical, if not a bit wild.
4. The unfinished and the imperfect often have greater appeal for me than the completed and the polished.
5. I must admit that I would find it hard to have a close friend whose manners or appearance made him/her somewhat repulsive, no matter how brilliant or kind (s)he might be.
6. A person should not probe too deeply into his own and other people's feelings, but take things as they are.
7. Young people sometimes get rebellious ideas, but as they grow up they ought to get over them and settle down.
8. Perfect balance is the essence of all good composition.

(Barron, 1958)

Take a break—cont'd

'Scoring': give yourself two marks for each answer that corresponds to those of a socially independent person, as shown below:

Question number	Socially independent person's answer	Your answer	Your score
1	True		
2	False		
3	True		
4	True		
5	False		
6	False		
7	False		
8	False		
Total			

The 'scale' is very simple. 0–6 is low, 12–16 is high.

Barron was trying to demonstrate that creativity was closely associated with independence of thinking and judgement. He interpreted his findings (42 people) as suggesting that socially independent people (high scorers) were more open to innovation, less demanding of symmetry and more accepting of imperfections . . . and more 'original' or creative in their thinking. It's a small group sample, so don't get too worried if you score low on creativity, but it could be interesting to try it out on the group you manage . . .

You will also find it useful to check out your understanding of the principles of 'creativity' by looking at the chapter by Bob Rawlinson, the CEO of the Edward de Bono Foundation in the UK. However you got on, the important point is to get feedback so you can judge how well you've done – even if it's only that it's best to leave it to others!

Anyway, if you really didn't do well, then use someone else – that's good management.

The same principle of the importance of feedback applies with regard to establishing and maintaining a relationship . . . but how do you *know* you've built up a reasonable/good relationship? Well obviously there's a contractual element involved with some colleagues (for example, facilities managers) which means you'll have some KPIs, but a 'good' relationship with the police may be different from that established with the catering company. However, there are some generic criteria which can be used . . . try 'ranking' the relationship (see box below).

Take a break . . . Ranking

Think of *one* relationship with a fellow professional and then answer the following questions with reference to that relationship.

1	Does this external professional colleague only visit school when you are there?	YES/NO
2	Is there good eye contact in conversations?	YES/NO
3	Do you both use appropriate forms of address in formal meetings?	YES/NO
4	Do you agree on everything?	YES/NO
5	When meeting this colleague, is the balance of conversation task-focused?	YES/NO
6	When talking to other staff, do you use formal title(s) in referring to this colleague?	YES/NO
7	Do you mix socially?	YES/NO
8	Does anybody else in the school talk to you about this colleague?	YES/NO
9	Have you had a (public) disagreement with this colleague about a work issue in the last 6 months?	YES/NO
10	Does (s)he attend other school events?	YES/NO

Scoring

Question	Professional	Social/Informal
1	NO	YES
2	YES	NO
3	YES	NO
4	NO	YES
5	YES	NO
6	YES	NO
7	NO	YES
8	YES	NO
9	YES	NO
10	NO	YES

Take a break—cont'd

Interpretation

Each question indicates a degree of professional vs social/informal relationship. For example, if the answer to question 8 is 'NO', then it is probably because you are perceived as being too close to that individual. This is not necessarily a good thing, as the perceived social/informal perspective may be preventing you receiving honest feedback from others.

If you 'connect' your responses, you will see an indicative profile which will give you an idea of the status of your relationship.

1.8 'You talkin' to me . . .?'

OK . . . so you've done your best . . . you've tried every trick in the book (this one!) and let's face it, the relationship isn't working . . . you're being taken advantage of and not getting what you want . . . so complain . . .

However, let's get this straight . . . complaining can bring out the worst in you (temper?), it is time-costly and stressful, so be sure you HAVE tried all the tricks. Also, do remember that *every* relationship goes through a number of identifiable phases and if you haven't realised which phase you're in, it can 'cut off' the relationship before it starts. One useful way of thinking is to adapt Alfred Tuckman's model relating to teams. He identifies four phases in team building – Forming, Storming, Norming and Performing. Think of these in terms of relationships; the Forming is the 'polite' first stage – but one we recommend you should focus on. The second phase, Storming, is the difficult one, as people realise and stress their own views. Eventually, they move to Norming, where acceptance of others' position is the 'norm', before moving to Performing. However, these are not all 'equal time' phases, and people can have different perceptions in phase two, with, for example, one person believing that they had already gone through this because of the time scale. In such cases, people can make the mistake of thinking the relationship has broken down, and act accordingly . . . usually leading to a complaint. However, if you are clear that the relationship has broken down, then don't be half-hearted – you have to see the complaint through.

So, before you make a complaint, think carefully about what you want to achieve, and don't fall into the trap of distraction. How often have you got into your stride in making a complaint, and said, 'and another thing'. The basics of 'good' complaining are straightforward and escalate as can be seen in the checklist below.

Example: Good practice in making a complaint

- when you've decided to complain – just do it, don't prevaricate
- arrange a meeting or telephone call to air the complaint
- mind your manners . . . don't be rude even if you feel it's justified
- check the facts, and stick to them . . . don't get personal
- keep the complaint simple by focusing on one point
- listen and recognize progress – if any
- if not satisfied, write and confirm the complaint

To illustrate the point, let's leave Alan alone . . . you two are doing OK, but there's a real problem with the educational psychologist . . .

- she doesn't come when she has arranged to
- she is rude to staff and occasionally refuses to deal with some individuals
- she hardly ever responds to emails and letters
- when she arrives at the school she complains about something every time (it's too cold, no tea was offered etc.)
- reports are often up to two weeks late
- she has, on more than one occasion, failed to support the school in discussions with parents

. . . the relationship hasn't broken down – it never existed! So it's time to complain . . .

Preparing to complain

Structure your complaint using the checklist. For example, which 'issue' will you focus on? Prepare a draft script outline and practise on someone not from your school.

1.9 Summary

What you've been given in this chapter are some generic principles, tools and techniques to establish a good working relationship with most people. However, it would be foolish to apply *all* the principles equally to every professional that you work with. Each of these colleagues has a different perspective and set of values. Empathy with each is certainly something to be worked at, and the work of Daniel Goleman on Emotional Intelligence (EI) is useful here. The key to good practice, as we recommend it, is to read the relevant chapter for each fellow professional and use the generic elements as a 'checklist', thus producing a template for each context. With practice (like all things) this gets easier!

But don't forget:

- build the relationship first
- be active, not passive in your relationships
- acknowledge differences in the motivation of other individuals and groups, and seek to manage these
- don't allow 'social roles' to determine your relationships, but do account for them
- there are huge pressures on us all to conform to social norms, tease out when these forces are positive and negative in their impact
- communication – we all know it, but it's worth restating, the way we communicate determines the types of relationship we establish

References and further reading

Barron, F. (1958), 'The psychology of imagination', *Scientific American*, 199, 150–66.

Goleman, D. (1998), *Working with Emotional Intelligence*. New York: Bantam Books.

Hay McBer Group (2000), *Research into Teacher Effectiveness*. London: Report to the DfEE – Research Report 216.

McLelland, D. C. (1961), *The Achieving Society*. Princeton: Van Nostrand.

NCSL (2000), 'Research into teacher effectiveness', report by Hay Mcber Group to the DfEE. London: Hay Group.

Tversky, A. and Kahneman, D. (1991), 'Loss aversion in riskless choice: a reference-dependent model', *Quarterly Journal of Economics*, 106, 1039–61.

Zajonc, R. B. (1968), 'Attitudinal effects of mere exposure', *Journal of Personality and Social Psychology*, 9, Monograph supplement No. 2, Part 2.

Useful websites

www.personalitypage.com/high-level.html: An interesting site for anyone wishing to explore personality types in greater depth.

www.socialpsychology.org: One of the largest internet sites devoted to psychological research and teaching. In these pages, you'll find more than 15,000 links related to psychology.

Creative Tactics to Successfully Build Relationships

Bob Rawlinson

2

2.1 Tactics to building successful relationships

You do not have to want to be successful. You do not have to value success. But . . . if you want to have successful relationships, then there are two attitudes you might adopt:

1. The first is the passive attitude, which tells you that there is nothing you can do except pray you have the right talent and temperament.
2. The second is the positive attitude, which tells you that that there are many things that you can do to create, develop and maintain a positive and lasting relationship. The positive attitude involves being ready for the relationship, spotting it, and making the maximum use of it – but not to sit around, waiting for it to happen.

So, knowing what you want to do, determination and persistence are very important. You will have to have these qualities as a strategy to establish successful relationships – but they can be learned and acquired. One useful way of acquiring the necessary qualities (for your discrete and individual personality) is to look at the dominant characteristics of successful people and try to categorize them into certain 'styles'. You can then use the categories to help organize your own behaviours and responses when dealing with such people in your workplace context – having set them against your own style and considered what's possible for you to change! The last thing you want to do is turn into Uriah Heep, becoming chameleon-like in dealing with people. That behaviour doesn't establish a successful relationship – it establishes a one-sided relationship!

So, the following sets out a suggested approach for building, and sustaining, an effective relationship and uses a 'style' approach. Before moving on, let's be clear that we believe this approach is more valid than the 'trait' basis of behaviour – 'I was born this way, so that's the way I am'. This approach means you may as well give up reading now if nothing can change!

2.2 Styles and characteristics of success

Successful people show a variety of styles, but is there one which, if adopted, would be likely to lead to success? The traditional image of success is that of a person who is strong minded, ruthless, and hardworking. However, when we look at the different 'success styles' it is not surprising that many people do not fit completely into these images.

2.2.1 The advertising creative style

Let us take a look at the way Alex Kroll, the president of the world's largest advertising agency, gets the best out of his creative team.

Kroll's style is to infuse his staff with enthusiasm, exciting their imagination, by involving them in a problem and arousing their creativity.

2.2.2 The retail management style

Another businessman's ability to get the best out of people also became crucial to his success. In 1982 Sir Terence Conran, designer/businessman chairman of Habitat and Mothercare, took a risk in establishing these two brands. He claimed that the idea was very simple, but other people had looked at similar ideas, had a go, and failed. Sir Terence claimed that it was because they didn't do it with enough conviction to make it a success. That is the difference.

People looked at it and said that this business is a terrible risk. But the very conviction of everybody working on the project from the designers to the shop floor staff, to the people who did the advertising and the people who manufactured the clothes, produced a totally inspired team effort. That total conviction, where every detail was in place because the team were convinced it was right, and went the 'extra mile' to ensure it worked, filled the public with a feeling of confidence.

Enthusiasm rubs off onto people, creating a 'can do' attitude and nothing will get in its way.

2.2.3 The inventor's entrepreneurial style

The inventor Sir Clive Sinclair acknowledges that he lacks both of the two previous styles. His success is due to thinking up new ideas – the pocket calculator, the digital watch, the home computer, his flat screen TV. There is no doubt Sir Clive Sinclair is a brilliant electronics genius, but the success and failings (C5s!) of the company are related to his personality . . . which is exceptional at thinking up new ideas and marketing them effectively. But then the challenges of the company are also related to his personality and indicate that he is not a manager either by inclination or by training. He is a fairly reserved person in some ways so can find it very difficult to cope with hundreds of people and therefore avoids general management as far as possible.

However, he still has a 'successful style', which is related to his boldness in concept and in business. This is the surprising boldness that is often to be found in someone who is rather shy.

2.2.4 The sports coach style

As one of the most successful coaches in world rugby union history, Rod MacQueen led the Wallabies to achieve an 'unbeaten ratio' of 81 per cent in his four-year coaching term.

At age 47, MacQueen assumed the role of national coach in 1997 after Australia had suffered a humiliating 61–22 defeat at the hands of South Africa, and by the time of his retirement in 2001, the Wallabies had won not only the Tri Nations and Bledisloe cup tournaments but had also brought home the most coveted prize of all – the World Cup.

In his book *One Step Ahead*, co-authored with Kevin Hitchcock, MacQueen reveals how he took the lessons he learned from life and from running his own business and applied them to coaching rugby teams. His challenge in turning around the Wallabies demanded radical change not only in the team but in the sport as a whole, all under intense media and public scrutiny.

A strong advocate of the thinking methods of Dr Edward de Bono, MacQueen is convinced that fresh, lateral thinking is the keynote of successful relationship building in the boardroom and on the playing field. He found plenty of opportunity in the tradition-bound sport of rugby to test that conviction. 'To be successful it was obvious we had to change. The perception is always that change is risky.' However as MacQueen notes, 'the greatest risk is staying the same.'

How can I use this?

The short answer is that it's useful because it's only got four categories, which is even more advantageous when you consider there is no one 'best' success style, so it's easy to imagine a 'mix'. This is optimistic point number one, and number two is that there is help on hand to learn and develop these styles in yourself to help 'mirror' behaviour – a key element of building a successful relationship. I would be foolish to claim that 'my' approach (the de Bono approach) is the only way – there are other approaches, just as there are other styles – but let me try and convince you that the de Bono approach is the best in terms of building and sustaining effective relationships. It starts with 'differences' – which are usually the cause of disruption of relationships.

2.3 Differences: The importance of perception

Dr de Bono's principle is simple. You have to see things from different perspectives, and these skills can be learned. In an argument you can have difficulty in seeing the other person's point of view. It comes down to three basic things:

- different information
- different perception
- different values

Once you can see where people come from, you can consider if the other person has better information and compare their values and perceptions to yours. You have to think: 'I am willing to listen.' As Edward de Bono argues, 'The purpose is to open up the mind and stop people from acting defensively.' The benefit of this approach has been embraced enthusiastically by both business and education with research completed by Michele de Bene at the University of Verona and Professor John Edwards at James Cook University, Australia. Further research is continuing under Sandra Dingli at the University of Malta in collaboration with a team of teacher-researchers from the Department of Education in Malta and the Edward de Bono Foundation UK based at Manchester Metropolitan University. All reaffirm the principles and the rationale . . . particularly that the majority of mistakes in ordinary thinking (outside technical matters) are mistakes in perception.

Our traditional emphasis on logic does little for perception. If the perception is inadequate, no amount of excellence in logic will make up for that deficiency. Perception is a matter of directing attention. If you are not looking in the right direction it does not matter how clever you are, you will not see what you need to see. Consider the example below.

Take a break . . . Directed attention

Consider this example: the terms 'right' and 'left' are spatial directions. North, south, east, west are also spatial directions. You can ask someone to 'look left' or to 'look south.' That instruction indicates a 'direction.' You look in that direction and see what you see, because your attention is 'directed' there. But you also have the ability to look in other directions – you're just not looking there – your attention needs 'directing' into other, different areas.

The Cognitive Research Trust (CoRT) programme devised by Dr de Bono to direct our thinking is divided into six parts of ten lessons each. The first part deals with 'broadening' perception. The fourth part introduces specific creative processes. In the first part, the 'attention-directing tools' (DATT) include: PMI, for a systematic scan of the Plus points, the Minus points and the Interesting points; OPV, for attention to Other People's Views; C&S for a deliberate focus on the Consequences and Sequel of a choice or action. The acronyms are necessary in order for the 'instruction' to exist in the mind as an 'operating concept'. Mere attitudes have no identity. These very simple tools are very powerful in their effect and can totally change initial judgements and perceptions.

2.4 Customer perceptions: What is a customer?

Every organization in the world – commercial and non-commercial – has customers. Now, I'm aware of the debate regarding 'schools as a business', but from my point of view, I regard somebody who pays me (directly or indirectly) for what I do, as a 'customer'. However, the number and type of customer is as varied as the possible number of 'success styles' interacting with the particular context of their value to your organization. In other words, innumerable!

Therefore every organization needs to identify its customers and ensure that it is in the business of meeting, and, surpassing their discrete needs. This may seem very obvious but before you can establish how to develop a good customer relationship you need to define not only what you believe your customer is, but who they are.

Have a go at the activity in the box below.

Take a break . . . The customer

1. Try to say in a sentence or two what you think is meant by your customer. Try to distinguish them from 'stakeholders' who may have an interest, but don't 'pay' you. Put their name in the first column.
2. How much (in monetary terms – pounds, euros, dollars etc.) is involved in the relationship, and is this payment direct or indirect? For example, in a school, you may bring in an educational psychologist for a consultation, but (s)he may be paid as part of a service agreement (indirect).
3. What's their 'success style'?

Take a break—cont'd

4. Now comes the difficult bit – how would you 'rank' your relationship on a scale of 1–5? One (1) being excellent, 5 being . . . well, you get the idea!

Customer	Value (indirect/direct)	Their 'success style'	Relationship ranking

5. Now ask, who . . .
   - is more likely to change attitude?
   - is in control of any change for the better?
   - (now) has a thinking framework (knowledge of styles) to help guide behaviours?

I'm not even going to answer the questions for you!

Building a successful relationship with an internal or external customer may not be easy or happen overnight, but if you have identified the need to change your thinking then your role is to ensure that it happens.

2.5 Reasons for relationship failure

Take a look at the following case study review of a failed business relationship (it doesn't matter what the business activity was, or whether it was public or private sector).

According to business people, the 'bad' points were . . .

- I had no clear direction or specific goals to achieve
- I believed my way was the only right way
- after 15 years I thought I had nothing to learn
- I did not listen to the criticism and views of others
- I blamed everybody else when something went wrong
- I fooled myself that I was working to help the relationship improve
- I did not use my time effectively to prepare for the discussion
- I got too friendly with the customer, making it hard to discuss difficult points
- I was influenced by negative remarks of others
- I did not look or act like a professional

According to the internal/external customer, the 'bad' points were . . .

- gave the impression they knew it all
- talked too much and asked too little

- appeared to be only interested in themselves
- knew nothing about the customers' needs
- had no enthusiasm for the job
- interrupted the customer
- was over anxious to get their point in
- reacted badly to the customers' suggestions
- did not come to the point quickly enough

There's a painful honesty from both sides, but the differences in perceptions are astonishing! As Stephen Covey succinctly puts it . . .

Seek first to understand then to be understood.

This 'thinking differently' about self needs to be addressed creatively. Simply taking feedback and trying to respond to discrete points will not suffice. You have to consider the 'meaning' behind each point . . . and . . . what the other person meant (or your perception of what they meant!). At this point you may be tempted to say, 'OK, thinking creatively may help me personally, but what will it do for the business?'

2.6 Creativity and the business sector

Let's just stop for a minute and think of the (possibly stereotypical) reactions you may get from putting those two words ('business' and 'creativity') together. Actually, you may even try the exercise! The common reactions we get are . . .

'You have to dye your hair and wear wacky clothes to be creative.'
'Creative people just sit around playing on their iPods all day.'
'You are creative if you work in the creative industry.'
'Creative people are difficult to control.'

Firstly, before you can think about 'getting staff to be creative', it is important to understand what true creativity is. The above statements are, of course, complete nonsense (well, maybe not the one about iPods . . .!). More seriously, perceptions and stereotypes exist because it is a human trait to pigeonhole people, but creativity comes in many forms and should not be thought of as a mysterious art.

We prefer to think that creativity means 'designing the way forward': that creativity is needed for change, improvement and ideas, and that without creativity there is only repetition and routine. In fact, we believe that creativity is as close to the heart of business as you can get. This is because all organizations are under pressure to find new and better ways to increase overall performance. Whether it's cutting costs, meeting targets or developing a new product or service, fresh ideas are in constant demand to remedy a problem or simplify a process.

Let's be honest, it's tough being in business today. In the first three years of business, DTI statistics show that 28.7 per cent of start-ups are likely to fail. There are, of course, many reasons for failure, however creative thinking will play a huge role in helping businesses to grow and be more profitable. According to statistics from the DTI, more than half (58.7 per cent) of employment in the UK is through small- and medium-sized enterprises (SMEs), so clearly it's an important industry sector. These businesses are more likely to thrive if they are unified, skilled and creative.

Dr. Edward de Bono, the world's authority on creative thinking, states: 'The quality of your thinking will determine the quality of your future.' So, how do you get staff to embrace creativity in their everyday lives and, more pertinently, will it help?

2.7 Lateral thinking

Creativity is not just about being a great artist or being able to play a musical instrument, it's also about taking an alternative approach to solving a problem. In the 1970s, Dr de Bono changed the world's approach to creativity when he coined the term 'lateral thinking'.

When looking to get a better understanding of the brain, Dr de Bono's research led to the discovery that the brain is a self-organizing system that routinely interprets inputs into patterns. The brain is not inherently designed to be creative. However, through the adoption of lateral thinking tools, it can be trained to move laterally across patterns, opening up new perceptions, concepts and ideas.

Dr de Bono has created formal techniques to help people break out from previously established thinking patterns and to foster lateral thinking. He proposes that 'the most effective way of changing ideas is not from outside, by conflict, but from within, by the insight rearrangement of available information.'

At this point, remember the box in section 1.3, and start to think about 'directed thinking' – only in this case, think 'self-directed' – more later!

2.8 Creativity and the public sector

The best minds are not in government. If any were, business would hire them straight away.

(Ronald Reagan)

Ronald Reagan was never shy to voice his opinion and this one could easily divide the private and public sectors. However, if there's one issue that unites government and businesses, it's the drive for improved performance. Whether it's cutting costs, meeting Gershon targets or simplifying complex processes, all key public services are under constant pressure to find new and better ways to increase overall performance. For schools who increasingly regard themselves as business-like, the distinction is probably irrelevant anyway!

As we enter the next phase of the information age, knowledge and its creative application will provide the key differentiator – from the way we educate our children to how we equip our staff with the skills to power the economy. The strength of our economy is partly related to having thriving and successful cities and towns, which only happens if schools and other educational institutions continually emphasize (self) improvement. If they can do this, then these places are more likely to thrive because they are unified, skilled and creative. However, to meet these ideals and yes, 'targets', we require a radically different approach . . . and we mustn't be afraid to link creativity to 'targets' or 'standards'.

2.9 So, why is creativity important?

David Miliband, as Schools Standards Minister, once said that 'standards and creativity go hand in hand.' Creativity means bringing into being something that was not there before. Creative thinking is necessary in every sector of business, whether in the public or private sectors. In short, we need it to solve problems, make improvements and create new opportunities.

Upon election to 10 Downing Street, Tony Blair called for senior government officials to be more creative, less hierarchical and to take more risks. The answer, to the credit of the Civil Service, was, 'this sounds great, but where do we start?' Dr de Bono was invited to help civil servants make better use of their collective minds. The aim was to move away from an adversarial approach, where meetings were used to score points, to a more constructive approach using de Bono' parallel thinking technique, Six Thinking Hats. In a simple experiment with three hundred senior civil servants, the introduction of the Six Hats method increased thinking productivity by 493 per cent.

2.9.1 Six hats

This technique puts everyone on a level playing field. Egos and tensions are removed from the equation as all participants are encouraged to think in the same, or parallel, direction at the same time by using the same thinking tool (the hat). Six Thinking Hats has been used successfully by world leaders, government departments, multinational corporations, miners and students and teachers in classrooms, providing an alternative to argument and allowing exploration instead of adversarial confrontation.

The practice is proven to improve relationships, reduce meeting times, increase productivity and encourage creativity. The six thinking hats (see box below) themselves are imaginary. The purpose of the technique is to modify a person's behaviour to increase creativity and to improve constructive dialogue. The goal is to think of as many points as all can under each kind of hat. This prompts the individual or the group to share all of their ideas rather than defend one point of view or another. For example: 'We will all put on the yellow hat and see if we can find some benefits to this idea.'

The hats

The red hat represents emotional thinking, intuition, opinion and hunches (subjective).

The yellow hat represents positive thinking: praise, positive aspects why it will work (objective).

The black hat represents critical thinking: criticism, negative judgement, why it will not work, caution (objective).

The white hat is purely the facts: information known and what further information is needed (objective).

The green hat is creative thinking: alternatives, new approaches and 'everything goes' (speculative/creative).

The blue hat represents the big picture, manages the thinking process, all the viewpoints (overview).

One of the key lessons from Edward de Bono's work is the removal of the mystery that surrounds creative thinking. Unfortunately, this seems to have penetrated global consciousness more than in the UK, where reports continue to surface that creativity is still viewed negatively by many businesses and that a dangerous creativity gap is opening up in the UK, which could take away its competitive edge. This negativity can be combated if creative thinking is more openly used and understood from an early age. Commenting on de Bono's work, Dr. Brian David, Nobel Prize winner in physics, says: 'Our culture is suspicious of any kind of thinking that works in ways other than through logic; and, to a very large extent, logical thinking is the only kind of thinking that is encouraged in our educational system' – however, this is improving. Dr de Bono's methods have been used by over 7.5 million children and students around the world and are mandatory on the education curriculum in many countries.

Oh, and in the UK? Well, as part of the government's 'New Deal' job finding programme, teaching youngsters with de Bono Thinking Systems for just six hours increased their employment rate by 500 per cent. In addition, UK government initiatives are placing more emphasis on encouraging and nurturing creativity at a young age and are starting to take effect. This supports de Bono's mantra that effective thinking, like literacy and numeracy, is not inborn: it has to be learned and practised to be effective. Children and students need to know how they learn as well as what they are learning. Yet, astonishingly, 50 per cent of organizations in the educational sector do not support the arts, and one in three will not look for qualifications which show creativity when recruiting, despite promoting its importance to young people in the classroom.

This is even more significant when you consider that the public sector is the biggest customer in the UK economy, so should be leading the way in driving innovation. Although it is no stranger to change, without creativity innovation will not be forthcoming and the public sector will continue to stagnate. Perhaps more significantly, local initiatives are increasing. This is probably because local authorities know their area and their citizens better than central government, and should not be afraid to introduce creative thinking practices to help prioritize and deliver local services and improve internal working processes.

2.10 Front-line staff will take the strain of change

Change is inevitable and with any new Prime Minister there are even more changes for front-line public servants to handle. But government improvement and marketing is about changing the attitudes and behaviours of everyone, both staff working internally within the public sector and the external target audience – the voters, business people, the school leavers and young children. The most effective way of achieving any level of change is by using innovative ideas to appeal and release the emotional triggers. By using creative thinking practices we can remove the mystery of creativity application, and it doesn't have to involve extra, 'new' resources. By thinking creatively about existing resources we can stimulate thought and innovation, which in turn will release previously 'unknown', spare capacity.

> There is no doubt that creativity is the most important human resource of all. Without creativity there would be no progress and we would be forever repeating the same patterns.
>
> (Edward de Bono)

2.11 A history of logical thinking

During the Renaissance, when Greek thinking infiltrated Europe through the influence of the Arabs in Spain, schools, universities and indeed 'thinking' in general, were in the hands of church people. These were people who did not subscribe to thinking which was perceptual, creative, or even constructive. To be fair, given their role, what they did need was truth, logic and argument to disprove heretics. So critical thinking became the core thinking. It was left for invention and design to be practised by individuals, and their evolution has, as a result, been very slow. Critical thinking is not enough. It is of course essential – just as the rear left wheel of a car is essential – otherwise the car doesn't move. Unfortunately, the prevention of errors is not sufficient. The brakes of a car are at their most effective only when a car is rolling forward or backward. But 'progress' needs the ability to design the way forward (and backward!), and this involves creativity. Without creativity there is only repetition and routine. Creativity is needed for change, improvement and ideas.

2.12 Embedding creativity in the workplace

All businesses and public sector organizations are under pressure to find new and better ways to increase overall performance. Whether this involves cutting costs, meeting targets, building relationships or developing a new product or service, fresh ideas are in constant demand to remedy a problem or to simplify a process.

So, how do you get staff to embrace creativity in their everyday lives and will it help? In the working world, we can learn a lot about creativity through humour. Comedians make us laugh by surprising us with a switch in perception. A funny joke is usually obvious in hindsight, but we need a bridge to help us get there. With lateral thinking however, there is no storyteller to make the jump for us. So we have to devise a practical means for cutting across the tracks. We can do this by using a combination of provocation and movement to produce the simple, but effective formula:

$$Provocation = Integration$$

Dr de Bono invented the word 'PO' which stands for a Provocation Operation. He says, 'It signals that what follows is to be used directly as a provocation (that is to say, used for its movement value). A PO provides some sort of value that has been provided historically by accident, mistake, eccentricity or individual bold mindedness. The PO (provocation) serves to take us out of the comfort of an existing pattern.'

An excellent example of PO in action is famously 3M's sticky Post-it notes. A company world-renowned for adhesives embarked on some lateral thinking and thought, 'We're a company known for sticking things, why don't we challenge that idea and make something that doesn't stick?' And the idea behind the Post-it note was born.

There are a number of approaches to PO, which are part of de Bono's thinking that help to encourage lateral thinking – for example, escape reversal, exaggeration, distortion, and wishful thinking. Using these methods, the lateral thinker is able to provoke their own thinking.

Whatever business you are in, lateral thinking is an essential means of fostering creativity. Unfortunately it doesn't happen overnight; like any skill it needs teaching and practising.

2.12.1 How do I start?

Obviously, the techniques need careful consideration, but there are a number of key 'principles' which can be useful to remember in any approach to creative thinking. These are set out below.

Creative thinking principles to successfully build a relationship

- perception is real even when it is not reality
- 'nothing' is the space for everything
- if you do not design the future someone or something will design it for you
- we may need to solve problems not by removing the cause, but by designing the way forward, even if the cause remains in place
- traditional thinking is all about 'what is'; future thinking will also need to be about what we can be
- effectiveness without values is a tool without a purpose

As education and businesses are faced with the many challenges ahead, this alternative approach will just make the difference . . . after all:

The quality of your thinking will determine the quality of your future.

(Dr Edward de Bono)

2.13 Summary

In this chapter we have taken what might be considered an unusual slant on relationships, but I am sure Dr de Bono would encourage us to do just that! The willingness to think creatively, which invariably means thinking positively, is a valuable attribute to those who are serious about relationship building.

Case studies of successful businessman tell us that there isn't one 'right' way of developing relationships. We do know, however, that perception is important, and in particular, that our customers' perception of us is their reality. Failure to recognize this may well lead to a failed relationship.

Using the techniques pioneered by Edward de Bono we can develop strategies to enhance our personal capacity to think creatively, and as a result, to create enduring and long lasting business relationships.

References

MacQueen, R. and Hitchcock, K. (2001), *One Step Ahead on the Field and in the Boardroom.* New South Wales: Random House.

Further reading

De Bono, E. (1967), *The Use of Lateral Thinking*. London: Cape Publishers.

De Bono, E. (1994), *Edward de Bono's Smart Thinking*. New York: Macmillan Audio.

De Bono, E. (2000), *Six Thinking Hats*. London: Penguin Books Ltd.

Useful websites

www.edwdebono.com/: The on-line Effective Thinking Course.

www.debonothinkingsystems.com/home.htm: de Bono Thinking Systems® is in the business of changing the way businesses think.

Part Two
The In-house Professionals

Administrators and Volunteers

Angela Harnett

3

3.1 Introduction

This chapter assumes that the reader is a member of, or works closely with, the School Business Team (SBT) – which may include the school business manager. It points out that administration is a 'profession' – established before many other areas of activity which now have that title – and therefore cannot be regarded as a generic part of other activities. Indeed, a recent Council for Administration (CfA) study revealed that 97 per cent of all employers state that business administration is critical to the effective function of their business and 40 per cent say they find it difficult to recruit suitably trained administration staff. Consequently, leaders and managers in learning centres need to consider building and maintaining appropriate relationships with regard to these staff in exactly the same manner as they would with, say, relationships with teaching assistants.

Administration is a title that covers a number of job roles including:

- customer care
- filing clerks
- account and wages clerks
- telephonists
- personal assistants

Obviously not all of these roles are present in separate individuals within every school (particularly small primary schools), but the roles themselves are very evident in all schools . . . sometimes even in one 'super-individual'! However, it is more normal for medium-sized primary and secondary schools to have several administrators, one of whom may be a volunteer.

There may be some initial puzzlement over this chapter: why would members of the SBT – especially SBMs – and also teaching staff (who are very familiar with administrative tasks) need to know how to manage other administrators – both within and external to the school? Well, part of the problem is that encountered by every other professional: teachers are not naturally good with other teachers, lawyers have similar problems with colleagues, doctors won't even go to other doctors when they're ill, and in universities, 'managing' fellow lecturers is so difficult that some higher education institutions have a rota which forces people to take the responsibility for managing other lecturers in turn! The rest of the problem lies in the necessary close working relationship between professionals working in the same activity area – so 'leaving it to the SBM' is not the answer.

The fact is that it is not simply a matter of 'telling' fellow administrators how to do things in order to get the best from these colleagues; there are some issues which are best explained by adopting the other person's perspective. This chapter will explore in depth some of the issues and will indicate how to get the best out of fellow administrators.

3.2 The legal context

It could be argued that administration has historically been seen in terms of secretarial work such as filing, typing, administration of systems, skills of making the boss's life easier. In more recent years the role has changed significantly, with administrators being involved in systems, communication, information and process management.

There are two principal agencies involved in promoting administration as a profession.

3.2.1 The Council for Administration

The Council for Administration is the national sector standard-setting body for business and administration. It is responsible for defining and promoting excellence in business and administration skills and practice across all industry sectors.

The CfA also performs research and has links with a number of countries. It is currently undertaking a project which benchmarks the UK Business and Administration Standards against both German and Australian standards.

3.2.2 The Institute of Administrative Management

Founded in 1915, the Institute is a company limited by guarantee; it also has registered charity status. Its charitable purpose is 'to promote and develop for the public benefit the science of administrative management in all its branches and to encourage the promotion and development of improved administration in offices'. It is important to note that School Business Managers (SBMs) form a substantial cadre of IAM membership. The Certificate and Diploma in School Business Management (provided by the NCSL) are accredited by the IAM.

As the role of SBMs is not yet fully set (there are 'standards', but these are not universally accepted), it is arguable that there can be such a thing as a comprehensive legal framework for the activities of administrators. Administrative staff rates of pay differ from organization to organization. Most administrators in schools linked to, for example, the local authority will have more formal terms of reference with a 'grade', accompanied by established terms and conditions, and a pay scale agreed in their local authority. However, as learning centres become divorced from such established contexts, the different conditions of service of people working within these contexts are beginning to cause tensions. Further, school business managers, who traditionally had different conditions from teachers and other support staff, are increasingly being assimilated into the senior leadership structure with commensurate rewards and the 'cascade' effect may be inevitable.

There is however, some good news for managers: there are national standards for administrators. These have been developed by the Council for Administration. It has also recently developed specific standards for SBMs. These standards however, are not legally binding in the same way that, say, medical standards are.

3.3 Key principles

Any function within an organization requires some form of administration: it is at the heart of an organization and without its efficient and effective use, organizations would stall. Schools could have the best teaching staff imaginable but ineffective administration would make their roles impossible. There are a number of areas that are important for effectively managing administration. These include:

3.3.1 Human Resource Management (HRM)

It is perhaps trite to say that managers need to be aware of the importance of people: it is perhaps more appropriate to say that they should be particularly aware of organization culture and how people are motivated. There is a tendency in dealing with administrators to think: 'these people like systems and processes, so they'll respond to a mechanistic approach.' This is a dangerous approach . . . machines don't 'bite' . . . administrators do!

More about this area of management activity later . . .

3.3.2 Administrative systems and processes

OK . . . they may be people, but . . . yes, they DO like systems and processes! To administrators, systems and processes are integral to the practice of administration. Systems-thinking plays an important role in understanding the contribution made by administrative processes to organizational effectiveness. Many teachers accept this for teaching, but not necessarily for the organizational support activities, and most administrators will have different views about the different systems and processes for different activities. Hence the dissonance in, say, the way photocopying is regarded by teaching staff and administrative staff. To understand these differences in your own organization, take a look at the box below.

Take a break . . . Difference is healthy!

1. List all the administrative tasks which will represent an 'interface' (however minor), between teaching and administrative staff.
2. Now ask teaching staff to 'rate' the activity as 'high/medium/low' (or numbered out of ten) in terms of the necessity for rigorous processes to be in place.
3. Ask administrative staff to do the same.
4. Before looking at the results, complete the exercise yourself.
5. Now compare the results . . .

Interpretation
Look for resonance and dissonance in order to judge effectiveness and efficiency.

Any activity where *all three perspectives resonate* (agree) can be regarded as an *effective* system and process, but you may wish to consider making the process more *efficient*.

Any activity where *none* of the three perspectives agree, is an area of dissonance. Something is wrong with the system/process if no one can agree on the importance of the process – it is neither efficient nor effective . . . start again!

Any activity where two of the three perspectives resonate is an area where you need to engage in discussion. It will usually be an activity which is *efficient, but not effective* from the third person's perspective. Photocopying is a classical example, with imposed limits on numbers or electronic permission systems a normal practice – but one which prevents, for example, an administrator or HLTA serving the teacher on (usually) a Monday morning!

3.3.3 Communication

Administrators regard information within an organization and the ability to organize, analyse and communicate this information (including quantitative and financial information) for 'the management' as a vital part of their job, so it's beholden on managers to similarly develop their skills in this area. There's nothing more dispiriting for an administrator than to hear a manager say, 'Oh, I really didn't need all this . . . but thank you anyway!'

All organizations must manage information, just as all commercial businesses must aim to make a profit. Information increases knowledge, reduces uncertainty and adds value when used.

Good decisions are virtually impossible without appropriate information and managers are constantly seeking more and better information to support their decisions.

3.3.4 Knowledge of financial and other resource management

As a member of the school business team, it is strongly recommended that you develop knowledge and understanding of the key principles involved in managing organizational resources and the tools and techniques associated with managing finance, projects and facilities. Such tools and techniques are becoming increasingly important in management decision making where rational and logical arguments are expected to justify any decisions made. You don't have to be an expert, but developing an appreciation of these 'dark arts' will help you get the best out of those who ARE the experts. A good example of this is the PRINCE 2 methodology for project management. The approach is rapidly becoming a requirement for managing government-funded projects, and limiting knowledge of the technique to *one* member of staff is not sensible.

3.3.5 Strategy

Administration covers a wide range of activities and processes essential for *both* the smooth running of the organization *and* in helping the organization to achieve its aims and objectives. There is a general misconception that, because it has a support role, administration affects only the operational level of the organization and therefore is essentially inward facing. Senior leaders need to remember that administration can be effective or . . . bureaucratic – which is essentially, poor administration, because it's operationally, rather than strategically, focused.

3.4 The reality

All of the above areas are important but when working with professional administrators in learning centres, human resource management and communication are the key skills that need to be utilized.

3.4.1 HRM

Centres of learning from different sectors (public/private, academies/centres of excellence, children's centres/nurseries etc.) have different levels of human resource management powers and responsibilities. However, all have HRM as a central function or concern. Consequently, it is important to consider the reasons why human resource management is so important and more specifically, the basic principles involved in the recruitment, selection and subsequent management of fellow administrative professionals. Recruitment and selection are relatively straightforward, with the CfA and the IAM offering ready-made guidance and standards. However, managing these professionals is a little more complex and involves knowledge and understanding of two key management areas – teamworking and motivation.

The diversity of organizations should not obscure the fact that all organizations share several key features, namely, people, objectives and structure. The interaction of people and objectives is the basis for an organization, structure provides a framework to coordinate and channel the efforts and interaction of people. These processes have to be effectively managed.

The keys to working with people in organizations are:

- generating a motivated, skilled and harmonious workforce
- generating commitment to the organization and its goals, objectives, strategies and organizational culture
- winning individuals' hearts and minds
- treating human beings as humans and not as a 'resource' or 'commodity'

One very effective way of combining all these elements is to promote teamworking as a culture . . . and then get the team to 'do it'! In schools this is an ideal rarely attained for several reasons . . .

3.4.2 Teamworking

Working with teams of people does not come naturally to all leaders, managers and administrators. Schools are relatively small organizations and inevitably some schools will work 'naturally' as one team. However, specific teams can usually be identified *within* most schools . . . and the basic, almost stereotypical identification is that of the teaching team and the administrative team. Unfortunately you have to accept that even this identification is fraught with problems – but is a pragmatic acceptance of the tendency of any minority group of people (administrators) to band together against the majority (teaching staff). If these teams are perceived differently – both internally (by the team itself) and externally (by the 'other' team) – then the effectiveness of each team comes into question. Working with teams involves working with the behaviours, interactions and personalities of team members. Working together across professional teams has to be managed carefully because each member is coming to the team with different perceptions and even a different vocabulary. Therefore accept that there will be an 'administrative team', and as a member of the SBT, aim for a consistent interpretation of what that means.

Questions to consider when thinking about setting up teams in your organization are:

- How are teams formed? Does my organization conform to any one approach?
- The purpose of the team? What is the aim – is it long or short term?
- What does the team do? What's the objective(s)?
- What makes an effective team? What KPIs are we going to devise and agree?
- What are the characteristics of a weak team? How do I know when it's going wrong?
- What are the implications of working in teams? What resources does the team need?

Fortunately, however, there are plenty of theories, books and courses to help you . . . my message is simple: use this questioning approach with the administrative team, and get the 'answers' recorded. Then distribute it to all members of the SBT, who will at least then have a common understanding of what the administrative team thinks of itself. It may seem to you now that teamworking is not worth it, but administrative management is now so complex, no one person can do all the tasks nor can activities exist in isolation.

3.4.3 Motivating the team

Unfortunately there's another element which follows the 'set-up' phase . . . getting the team motivated. One of the key roles of any leader or manager is the task of motivating individuals and teams towards the achievement of organizational (and individual) objectives and strategies. The task of motivating involves having responsibility for promoting individual and team performance, commitment to the organization and encouraging overall job satisfaction while in the workplace. However, motivating people is not an easy task! Many people join organizations to satisfy their own wants and needs and, in that respect, may be more interested in satisfying their own personal goals than those prescribed by managers. As this is the case, managers may use an understanding of what motivates people to monitor and control their performance so that they work harder and become willing participants in the drive to make the organization more efficient and effective.

Many people associate motivation with their wages or salary or other financial incentives that they receive. They view pay as having a direct impact on their ability to have a decent standard of living and the ability to satisfy other needs. However there are other motivators such as the job and recognition that motivate people. Again, there are many theories, books and courses to help gain this knowledge and understanding – but my recommendation is to take a look at the seminal 'stuff' such as Maslow and Hertzberg to help convince you that money isn't everything!

3.4.4 Communication

Communication within any organization is vital, but unfortunately organizations usually rely on one form because it's part of the culture. Thus organizations concerned with technology usually focus on emails, whereas the meetings of sales teams have almost legendary status for unusual 'interactions'! Learning centres are no different: therefore, as administrators usually work with text, the 'document' approach is most common – memos or emails.

Unfortunately, because schools are places of human beings, then leaders, managers *and* administrators need to develop the skills of variety in communication. Communication is involved with people (and in this case, two very different sets of people) therefore the elements of perception, misinterpretation and hearing what you want to hear, are part of this process – and that's why leaders have to stress it's a two-way process. As I pointed out above, although communication is one of the 'big two', there are other elements involved here (for example, systems-thinking), so administrators also have a responsibility to make communications work, and as can be seen below, the business of teams is again very relevant.

In order to develop clear and effective communication systems within learning centres there needs to be a clear plan of the:

- communication taking place
- methods of communication
- skills to be developed

However cohesive a team may be, there are times when conflict occurs. This might be through competition between members, a breakdown in communication, high task dependence on members, or a clash of personality. Communication is the key to conflict resolution. The following approach to communication can help with conflict resolution and avoidance of conflict in the first place:

- gathering the facts
- engaging in discussions to agree the cause of the problem

- being open about the conflict by recognition of the 'differences'
- encouraging dialogue about the conflict
- using mediation from a third party

It is important that conflict does not go unchecked. If it does, it may lead to inefficiency and disruptions in productivity.

3.5 Communicating with . . .?

The SBT (and especially the SBM) will have to work with their administration team and other professionals external to the school. The school team might be people specifically appointed to roles such as accounts clerk, administrator or facilities manager, and might also include people who are part-time, recently returned to work, or volunteers. Taking each of these in turn . . .

3.5.1 People appointed to a specific role

These people will usually be highly qualified in their own field which in itself can cause tensions. Leaders need to set clear guidance that they are the 'manager' in terms of responsibility but simultaneously recognize the value of having experts in their field. The key lies in one aspect of communication: the reporting structure within the school needs to be clear. Each particular member of the SBT will need to communicate clearly that (s)he may have conversations with the accounts clerk and facilities manager but these professionals report to (usually) the SBM.

3.5.2 Part-time staff

Part-time workers often feel they do not belong within organizations because they miss out on part of the week. The SBT needs to find ways of keeping them informed about what is going on in the school and make sure they are included in all events even if they are on days that the person does not work – back to the motivation stuff!

My recommendation is to ensure that this group of staff have specific tasks to perform on the days that they are in the school. Ideally they should be tasks that happen on these particular days, for example collection of money. It might take extra organization to initially accommodate this group but if they feel a task belongs to them they are more likely to take ownership and develop it.

3.5.3 Recently returned to work

It may be stereotyping, but many administration staff in schools are mums who have recently returned to work. The SBT needs to motivate these staff without being intimidating or conversely, intimidated! They might find themselves in a situation where the returner to work has an expectation that (s)he can act as the senior manager they perhaps were before they left their previous jobs! In both events the SBT needs to have strategies such as:

- get to know how these people prefer to function
- find out motivations – specifically, those related to the role
- develop some team building exercise
- make the boundaries clear at the outset (preferably by example)
- give people responsibility which is documented

This group will need clearly defined jobs from the first day and they might need a high level of supervision for some time. However, once they have settled into the role many of these people can become huge assets to the organization as they are given more responsibilities and are able to problem solve for themselves.

3.5.4 Volunteers

It could be said that volunteers within administration are a recent phenomenon. Schools have tapped into the volunteer market for classroom activities for years, which is interesting when you realise that many of the parents, mums in particular, are more likely to have held a job that involved administration in the private or public sector rather than teaching. In effect, using them in administration is a more effective use of resources.

This group could be a joy to work with, or a nightmare. Perhaps one of the reasons for past reluctance in using volunteers in an administrative role was confidentiality. Volunteers need to be carefully inducted into the role and given clear boundaries about confidentiality, but it is a two-way process: the expectations for these roles are determined by the amount of time people can give to the school. In order for this to work well there need to be clear:

- time frames
- expectations
- jobs to be completed

The types of jobs this group could be expected to do include: collection of money, ordering stock, filing, typing and reception. The issue here is that *both* parties may feel these tasks are 'add-ons' to the mainstream activities of the school. The key lies in communicating to all staff that the individual is part of the school (and made to feel so) and should be recognized for the work they are doing.

One way of doing this is to use qualifications and accreditation. Financially supporting professional development (for example, the Certificate of Administrative Practice) can be a powerful motivator for this group.

3.6 Preparation and planning for immediate effectiveness

One issue with these groups of administrators has been the time it takes (as, for example, a part-time worker) to become effective. However, this is no reason not to make the effort. There are three generic issues that these groups need information and training for:

- induction that covers policies and behaviours
- how to deal with the stakeholders
- managing the telephone system

By focusing on these relatively straightforward activities, Senior Business Teams can secure *immediate* additionality from administrators.

3.7 Induction that covers policies and behaviours

People who are working in school administration need to be aware of how the school functions, where the stock is kept, when and where they take a break. They also need to be aware of some of the school policies related to children. This would include child protection and behaviour management. They also need to know about the school ethos and what is acceptable and what is not. Many of these people will have children of their own but they will need some input on how to talk to children, how they should dress for the job and so on. Things which full-time staff might take for granted need to be communicated in depth so that there are no misunderstandings, and you can even 'refresh' your existing Induction Programme by innovative thinking: look at the box below.

Take a break . . . The innocent eye

Why not ask a colleague from another school to 'swap' administrators for a day – with the full purpose of recording all the differences. This 'innocent eye' approach can pay dividends to both organizations in terms of both induction and identifying inefficiencies. 'Why do you do that in that way?' can be a challenging method of questioning processes!

3.7.1 How to deal with the stakeholders

There are a number of stakeholders within school life. These include:

- children
- parents
- teachers
- governors
- local authority members
- Ofsted inspectors
- health professionals
- police

. . . and many others.

Administrative staff need to be aware of these different groups and their roles in relation to the school. They also need to be given guidance on how to deal with these people when they come into contact with them and whom they should refer them to if their manager is not available.

3.7.2 Managing the telephone system

Many people assume that answering the telephone is easy. However for some-one entering a new environment this simple task could be quite intimidating. It is good practice to give each new member of the team a short lesson in:

- how the system works
- the language to use when answering the telephone

- how to store information from a telephone conversation
- what to do with the information they have received

3.8 Professionals from outside the organization

This group of people might include local authority advisers or administrators, police, health workers, social services, builders and many others. When members of the SBT meet these different groups they need to be aware that communication is a key factor. This group of people do not necessarily understand the language of school. For example, what *is* the Foundation Stage? Some of these roles will involve health and safety and child protection. Because of the very nature of this there needs to be constant checking that there is a common understanding. For example the phrase:

Make sure the cable is safe.

. . . might mean to you that cable needs to be securely fixed to the floor so that pupils cannot trip over it. However, to the youth worker it might mean they just have to push it to the edge of the corridor! Other chapters in this book deal more specifically with these other professionals, so I'll content myself with saying that administrators in local authorities are . . . no different! Therefore treat them as you would your own.

Case study: Developing the team

The school is a small, voluntary aided church school with 209 pupils. The school has high expectations and high standards from all stakeholders. It gives a warm welcome to all visitors. The school takes the safeguarding of children, through risk assessments and CRB checks, very seriously.

The SBM developed a strategy within the school which included:

- part-time mums
- school experience students
- job seekers
- volunteers

The key to this experience was organization and looking at the skills people had. Each person was given a role that played to their strengths. They were all given on the job training in areas such as:

- how to answer the telephone
- confidentiality
- what they should be dealing with and what they should not be dealing with

This particular school has developed an excellent programme of CPD which includes in-house courses and NVQs. Both the school and the people involved in administration have benefited from this.

However, in terms of developing the team, the key was to ask each other to evaluate another team member's *strengths*. The exercise led to a greater appreciation of what others contributed to the team.

3.9 Summary

This chapter shows that there are a number of different administrators/professionals whom leaders work with. Some of these professionals need to be managed directly; some need to be managed indirectly within teams. However, it is worth remembering that all of these groups have specific needs . . . treat each group and individual within their own context is the best advice I can give.

Further reading

Wendel, F. C., Hoke, F. A. and Joekel, R. (1995), *Outstanding School Administrators: Their Keys to Success*. London: Greenwood Publishing Group.

Useful websites

www.cfa.uk.com: The Council for Administration (CfA) is the leading authority in business and administration skills in the UK. It sets standards for administrative management across all sectors of the economy in England as well as providing training programmes.

www.instam.org: The Institute of Administrative Management (IAM) provides training in administrative management to all sectors of the economy. Membership is open to all those who work in this field.

www.tda.gov.uk: Training and Development Agency for Schools (TDA). The TDA website provides much useful information on professional development opportunities for support staff working in schools and includes guidance on performance management.

http://volunteers.uea.ac.uk/projects/vips/index.php: This is a useful website hosted by the University of East Anglia (UAE) It provides guidance on the use of volunteers in primary schools (also known as VIPs).

4 Teaching Assistants

Joy Coulbeck

4.1 Introduction

This chapter explores some of the issues facing members of the School Business Team (SBT) in relation to the management of support staff in the classroom, particularly Teaching Assistants (TAs). There are two essential dimensions to this field, exemplified by the UK context. First, the overarching strategy driving an ever-widening workforce to achieve higher standards of pupil achievement (TDA, 2006a), and secondly, the operational issues that managing the growth of the school workforce presents for school leaders.

Significant levels of funding have been put in place to create jobs for teaching assistants and HLTAs along with funding for new training programmes to support them. The growth in numbers of classroom support staff has been rapid and marked.

Since 1997, the number of support staff working in schools has nearly doubled. Department for Education and Skills (DfES) full-time-equivalent figures show a 97 per cent increase in the number of support staff between 1997 and 2005, from 136,500 to 268,600. This compares with an 8 per cent increase in the number of teachers over the same period. DfES figures suggest one of the fastest growing groups over this period is teaching assistants (TAs) (61,300 to 148,500), which includes special educational needs (SEN) staff (24,500 to 48,100).

(TDA, 2006a).

Provisional figures for 2006 show that the number of support staff has more than doubled since 1997 and now tops 287,100. Table 4.3.1 charts the rise of these numbers and as schools witness this unprecedented expansion of TA numbers, they are becoming aware that for the first time teachers may not constitute the majority group within the staff of the school.

This influx of extra teaching assistants in schools has changed the balance within the school workforce, and with this change has come complexity and uncertainty both for teaching assistants and their managers alike. This chapter seeks to explain some of the ambiguities and tensions and suggests a model of approach against which to measure current practices.

4.2 Legal context

The international legal framework under which teaching assistants operate is not clear-cut. The context for individual schools is probably best determined by the answers given to the question: are teaching assistants professionals? Those who count themselves members of the 'Baby Boomer' generation will remember how, not so long ago, the debate raged about whether teachers themselves were professionals (*The New York Times*, 12.04.1988). In the job creation scheme in the USA in the 1960s the term *paraprofessionals* emerged and it appears to sit comfortably between education professionals and the many descriptors of support staff (Watkinson, 2003). Regarding teaching assistants as paraprofessionals may help to consolidate their role and status within the workforce, and will enable us to consider how SBMs may ensure that the management of them is secure and consistent.

4.3 The growth of 'a thousand flowers'

The UK government is committed to the expansion of the school workforce – and for good reason. Successive government initiatives and

Table 4.3.1 Growth in numbers of teaching assistants and teaching support staff in LA maintained schools in England

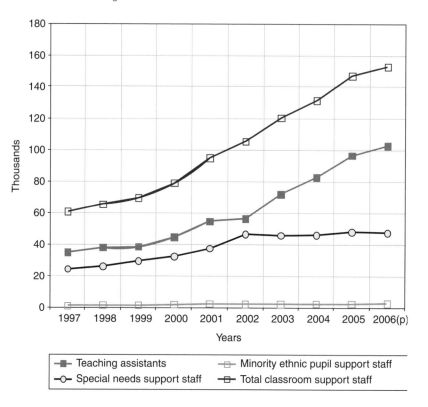

Source: Annual School Census 2006

legislation have been implemented with the aim of improving the services that schools offer children and maximizing the skills base of the workforce: the 'Remodelling the Workforce' agenda, the '14–19 Education and Skills' strategy, Extended Schools and 'Every Child Matters' agenda are prominent among these. Of particular relevance to what we are considering in this chapter is the 'Remodelling the Workforce' agenda which was introduced under a National Agreement (2003) entitled 'Raising Standards and Tackling Workload'. This was a policy initiative to provide:

> Teaching assistants and Higher Level Teaching Assistants (HLTA) to take over a wide range of administrative and secretarial tasks from teachers. When fully

implemented, it provides for cover to allow teachers to spend 10 per cent of their
time to carry out planning, preparation and assessment (PPA).

(TDA, 2006e:183).

Teacher unions strongly resisted the introduction of the new role of Higher
Level Teaching Assistants (HLTAs), claiming that their role was encroach-
ing upon that of teachers and that consequently the role of the teacher was
being devalued (Watkinson, 2003:6; TES, 12.08.2005). So that although the
claim is that 'support staff are making a difference to virtually every aspect
of life in a school' (TDA, 2006a:8), relationships between TAs/HLTAs and
teachers were, and could still be, potentially problematic. The fact that teachers, headteachers and governors alike routinely refer to support staff as 'non-
teaching staff' only serves to highlight the work that needs to be done in
restructuring the roles in schools and redrawing the lines of professionalism
and paraprofessionalism.

The legal situation is further obscured by the astonishing rise in new job
titles and roles – an ever expanding range of different job descriptions for
twenty-first century school communities: in addition to the new HLTA role,
we now have Learning Support Assistants, Bilingual Teaching Assistants,
Behaviour Support Assistants, Special Needs Assistants, Learning Mentors,
Resource Integration Support Assistants, Modern Foreign Language
Assistants, English as an Additional Language Assistants, Special Support
Assistants, Welfare Assistants (Balshaw and Farrell, 2002; TDA, 2007) – and
so the list grows. This is a phenomenon that Campbell (2005) describes as letting 'a thousand flowers bloom' (Campbell, 2005:153). Who will sow the seeds
of true growth? Who will order the potential chaos? Who will recruit safely,
induct and manage performance? Who will ensure that these new roles bear
fruit? Who will organize the training and development? Who will organize
the line management and deal with capability? This is a heavy responsibility
in terms of human resource management which clearly requires the skills of
an effective, well trained manager.

4.4 Who should manage teaching assistants?

There are two clear options: a senior teacher or a School Business Manager
(SBM) – but whoever is chosen, (s)he should be a member of the school

business team. However, one of the roles (SBM) is in itself a new role which has attracted much attention but some scepticism. However, the overwhelming evidence from NCSL is that the impact of this role is impressive (NCSL, 2007). School Business Managers (SBMs) have in recent years increasingly claimed their place within senior leadership/management/business teams and have a critical role to play with the effective deployment and management of the support staff in schools. The 'SBM as TA manager' is the adopted perspective in this chapter, but this is not to ignore the essential interrelationship (s)he has with the headteacher, senior and middle leaders in the teaching staff. It is recognized throughout that many decisions are joint decisions between these roles. Whether schools create the post of school business manager is a matter for individual schools to decide. The point is that a fully qualified and empowered SBM has a pivotal role in the management of TAs as a resource in schools, *in conjunction with* senior teacher leaders. It is assumed, therefore, that the line management of TAs is a system that is interlocked with teachers and their curriculum delivery needs – indeed an example of system leadership which can achieve more than the sum of its parts (O'Leary and Craig, 2007).

Although the theme of this chapter relates to the school business manager managing TAs, this is not necessarily the norm. One of the key questions facing schools today is whether leadership is distributed throughout the organization and who is empowered to contribute to the effective and efficient running of the school (Bennett *et al.*, 2003). TAs are frequently assigned to a particular teacher or class and it is assumed that the teacher will then manage the TA. Some schools regard the SENCO as the line manager of TAs where the prime function of the TAs is to support children with special educational needs (SEN). If the SBM is to have a clear role in TA management, there clearly needs to be good liaison and communication with key teacher roles.

One powerful argument in favour of the 'SBM as TA manager' model is that of empathy. NCSL, O'Sullivan *et al.* (1999) and Keating and Moorcroft (2006) have written about the rise of the school business manager, and SBMs who have gained professional awards through the National College for School Leadership will be well aware of the struggle to transform long-held assumptions about their role in order to become fully empowered, therefore they are well placed to understand the impact of the restructuring of the school workforce and the similar struggle to gain recognition that TAs are currently experiencing. Given the relative cost of human labour in *any* organization (public or private), the imperative is simple – more effective Human Resource Management (HRM). In schools, this is clearly guided by one simple term of reference: effective HR means teachers can teach within effective teams of professionals and paraprofessionals working alongside one another, each exercising their own leadership and each being fully supported with an effective system.

The two strands – the *Human* strand and the *Resource Management* strand – provide a model with which to identify the challenge for the SBM in managing TAs. The *Human* strand emphasizes the need to manage people: the need to understand and value the contribution that TAs make even though they are some of the lowest paid workers in the public sector (O'Brien and Garner, 2001). It also requires the manager to be conscious of the impact on the individual of complex and sometimes unclear systems which may result in conflict, lowered performance and even health issues.

The *Resource Management* strand presents both opportunities and threats – opportunities to raise pupil achievement through effective and innovative deployment of TAs, opportunities for better career and skills development through flexible school structures and quality systems for training and development. Whereas there may be threats to job security through variable funding and pupil movement, threats to school relationships as boundaries become indistinct and threats to salaries through redefining of roles.

Whoever manages must also operate on two levels – *strategic* and *operational*. Strategically, early twenty-first century schools exist and evolve in a highly charged, high-level atmosphere due to the current raft of governmental and societal agendas and initiatives coupled with increasing pressure on schools to improve. The most effective SBTs (which include the SBM) will be immersed in strategic thinking and planning. The effective deployment of TAs to deliver teaching or pupil support is a highly strategic factor, offering flexible ways of targeting support where and when it is most needed. The traditional paradigm of teaching assistants being largely employed in the Foundation stage or Key Stage 1 phase is now challenged by a view of strategic deployment of TAs across all school phases for wide ranging, targeted support.

Operational management encompasses the day-to-day functioning of the school and office systems. It is about the delivery of planned tasks and projects, gathering data, reporting on outcomes and solving problems as they occur. It is characterized by routines and processes and often driven by urgency. It deals with detail rather than the bigger picture, and can be very time consuming. Covey (1989) cautioned against the 'tyranny of the urgent', quoting Hummel (1967) who was referring to the interference of the telephone in modern day working life. How much this has worsened over 40 years! The point is that in the 'noise' and clamour of day-to-day routine urgency, the danger is that the bigger issues which were of greater importance are not heard.

These strands and levels constitute a matrix (Table 4.4.1) for SBTs who wish to analyse the management of TAs (strategic perspective) prior to working out approaches for day-to-day management activities (operational perspective).

The analysis shows the importance of the strategic dimension of TA management, but asks the question: do operational issues dominate if the School Business Manager is the responsible person? This is a real concern because while it is recognized that operational procedures need to be efficient and

Table 4.4.1 Model of strategic and operational functions relating to the management of teaching assistants

Human	Resource
Strategic	
• Safer recruitment	• HLTA/TA competencies
• Secure induction system	• Audit of skills base
• Mentoring and coaching	• Flexible deployment of TAs – SBM in
• Effective teams	conjunction with SMT targets TA resources
• TAs recognized as paraprofessionals	on a needs basis
• Performance management structure	• Enhanced opportunities for individual
• CPD to improve the skills base	skills-based contribution
• Career structure	• New pay structure
• Quality	• Total Quality Management (TQM)
	• Impact on pupil achievement
Operational	
• Line management	• Payroll
• Day-to-day communication	• Records of attendance and training
• Clarity of roles	• Resolution of contractual issues
• Relationships	• Conditions of work
• Training	• Sickness absence management
• Managing conflict	• Timekeeping
• Resolving issues between teaching staff and TAs	
• Giving advice	
• Discipline and capability	
• Return to work interviews	

effective, there can be no doubt that the greatest impact of the quality of management of TAs is at the strategic level. Watkinson (2003) states:

> The school therefore needs to review the qualities of its TAs and their deployment in order to best serve the aims of the school, the needs of pupils and teachers and the demands of the curriculum. These suggestions will involve the support of teachers and managers, affecting timetabling and other human and material resources.
>
> (Watkinson, 2003:10)

. . . which underlines the principles offered in Table 4.4.1 and summarizes the overall direction of this argument.

4.5 Managing teaching assistants – reports from the 'coalface'

Thirty school business managers studying for a BA (Honours) degree in School Business Management at Manchester Metropolitan University provided the author with data relating to how they currently manage TAs within their organizations. This preliminary small-scale research revealed that less than a third of this group were actual line managers for TAs, although the reality was that TAs looked to SBMs for a great deal of management, advice and support. Deputy heads, SENCOs or headteachers themselves were line managers of TAs, and in two cases a senior HLTA had been appointed to this role. Line managing TAs is certainly a potential role for the SBM if not an actual one because the picture that emerged from this group was that, whether line manager or not, a significant amount of time was given to TAs and their concerns on a daily basis (Table 4.5.1). It can be seen that more than half this group of SBMs spent half an hour or more on average per day with TAs, which is a significant cost in terms of SBM resources.

This is, however, a snapshot view (and therefore no generalizations should be made), and it is argued that the way SBMs spend time liaising with or managing TAs is dictated by school systems and procedures.

Nevertheless, further reports from the BA students revealed the following perceptions of the concerns that they felt that TAs had:

- lack of recognition
- no 'voice'

Table 4.5.1 How much estimated time 30 SBMs spend per day in relation to managing teaching assistants

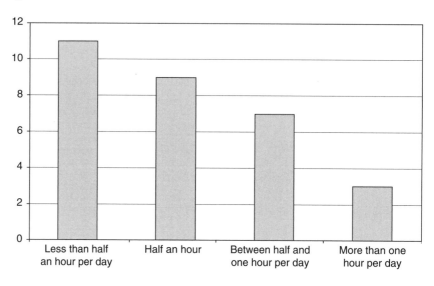

- lack of job description
- no performance management system
- inadequate line management
- lack of clarity about roles and responsibilities
- poor pay
- poor conditions of work
- poor treatment by teaching staff
- nobody to approach with problems
- social problems with groups within school

Of this list, the overwhelmingly highest priority of concern was *poor pay*, followed by *lack of recognition, being treated poorly by teaching staff* and *no 'voice'*. The congruence of three of these factors reveals to school leadership in general, and SBMs in particular, the focus of a common problem. What appears to be the case is that large numbers of poorly paid TA posts have been introduced quite rapidly, but not subsumed into flexible school structures. Instead they have been inserted into existing regimes without proper staff development for teaching staff or other members of staff as team leaders. O'Brien and Garner have written about the views and concerns of TAs and evidence on TA online forums bears testimony for the frustration and

Table 4.5.2 Causes of contact between SBMs and TAs

disaffection felt by some (www.teaching-assistant.co.uk). Watkinson also states:

> The issues are still there for schools, of professional boundaries, supervision and management, with the need for more explicit expectations and rationale for employment.
>
> (Watkinson, 2003:34)

. . . and she goes on to recommend a strategy for auditing and observing TAs in school in order to provide the manager with information about TA deployment and what 'hard and soft' outcomes of their work may be, where hard outcomes relate to measurable data and soft outcomes refer to less measurable but no less important human resource outcomes such as values, ethos, esteem, and personal development.

The MMU group of SBMs supplied information about what caused contact between TAs and SBMs and what need there was for management of them at the current time (Table 4.5.2). The evidence of operational concerns is overwhelming:

Pay and contractual issues dominate these meetings but the need to resolve conflict, solve problems, and to liaise with teachers and senior management is also high. The whole picture is one of issues, conflict and problems, presenting a complex and time-consuming human resource issue. Where such uncertainties and complexity abound there can be great wastage of time and resources. If TAs are approaching SBMs because they are unclear about their duties or responsibilities, or because they are being treated poorly by teaching staff, then there can be little expectation that the system is delivering the quality of support that it has the potential to deliver. Moreover, the drain on the SBM's time and energy in resolving these uncertainties and problems cannot be cost-effective. If this situation were to be as widespread as anecdotal evidence on TA websites suggests, then it may well be that the results of the massive investment in the TA role is falling short of its potential.

4.5.1 The SBM's formal involvement with TAs

There is therefore a strong argument for SBMs to propose, in their schools, that they have a more formal role with regard to TAs. The trained school business manager could:

- undertake a review of where TAs are deployed and how they are managed
- be the instigator of a team building strategy to realign the paraprofessionals with the professionals
- achieve better working practices in terms of clarity, quality, effectiveness and accountability
- perhaps most importantly, as the 'snapshot' above indicates, the SBM could enhance communications
- provide an invaluable service to the school through effective handling of several essential processes and systems to ensure the right TAs in the right job at the right time

Table 4.5.3 offers a model for these interlocking processes. Through joint strategic planning at senior management level, along with the effective

Table 4.5.3 Processes for management of teaching assistants

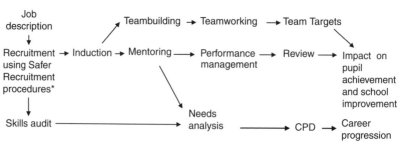

DfES 2007

analysis of data from the classroom, the SBM knows what types of TA are required and in what numbers, and can implement a smooth set of systems to ensure good quality employees are available and deployed effectively.

4.6 Issues

The aim of implementing the above processes is to ensure that the school employs high quality TAs in the school workforce and that this group of employees is seen as a valuable strategic resource. What follows are some key questions relating to the processes involved for the SBM to consider. These are set out in a questionnaire at the end, and the answers to each will dictate whether or not the SBM feels (s)he can take on this management role.

4.6.1 Safer recruitment – are the guidelines in place?

There can be no effective deployment of paraprofessionals in schools without the knowledge that everything that can be done has been done to safeguard children from adults who may harm them. Fortunately the most rigorous processes ever available are now implemented by the government and the national rollout of training is ongoing at the time of writing. Following the Bichard report of 2004, schools and their governing bodies must ensure that guidelines have been followed and that all possible steps have been taken, however it is worth mentioning that however robust these recruiting procedures are, they cannot form an absolute guarantee that no unsuitable person will escape the vetting and barring procedures, which are to be in place in the autumn of 2008. Every school is required to undertake the training and make sure that key members of staff understand how these guidelines affect them.

4.6.2 Induction – is the system effective and how do we know?

No school should be without an effective induction system for new members of staff. The investigation by MMU SBMs paints a varied picture, however. One of the main problems with induction systems for complex organizations is information overload. While some schools did not have an up-to-date induction pack, some commented that there was no 'follow up' after the induction period.

4.6.3 Mentoring – what contribution could the introduction of mentors for new TAs make to the quality of work achieved and is this cost-effective?

Matthews (2003) has written in detail about the use of mentors in educational institutions. Among the definitions that she has gathered lies a simple definition of a mentor from Reece and Brandt (1993) who say that 'Mentors are people who have been where you want to go in your career and who are willing to act as your guide and friend.' On the other hand she cites Lacey (1999) who states that 'A mentor is a trusted and significant leader who works with a partner (a mentee) to help them learn things more quickly or earlier, or to learn things they otherwise might not have learnt.' (Matthews, 2003:314) This latter definition briefly summarizes the purpose of a mentor and suggests that there would be a benefit to this role. It would speed up the induction process, contribute to team building and at the highest level ensure that the values, culture and ethos of the school are communicated at a deep personal level.

4.6.4 Skills audit and needs analysis – what are the TA's strengths and weaknesses? How does the TA regard this picture? Are there any special skills that may be developed to increase the services that the school provides?

These are good questions for the reflective practitioner (Schön, 1991) and any new practitioner benefits from such reflection and review. The needs analysis is also a vital starting point for the CPD/performance management cycle as well as providing essential information for good quality deployment.

4.6.5 Team management – do we have recognizable teams for delivering teaching and learning within school and do TAs feature as part of these teams? Is their membership recognized and do they belong? Who leads these teams and to whom are they accountable?

The series of questions again points to an audit that goes beyond the para-professionals but emphasizes the need to establish the location of roles and responsibilities and moreover is a call to end the uncertainty surrounding TAs' status and job roles. Work to establish the remit of existing teams or the formation of new multi-professional teams would need coordination and resourcing, and the SBM can clearly have an impact here. Wood *et al.* (2007) suggests that the SBM has a pivotal strategic role in rationalizing this problem:

> In larger schools a hierarchy of support staff is evolving, often with the school business manager leading a team of staff.
>
> (Wood *et al.*, 2007:12)

The key word is *evolving*: schools hierarchies are repositioning themselves to adapt to the wider, more diverse workforce. It would be reasonable to suggest that some schools are adapting better than others.

Whatever stage an individual school is at, teams will only function well if a balance of roles is achieved and SMART targets set so that all team members function well together, fully aware of the tasks in hand and the timescale within which the targets should be achieved. DSBM award holders will be familiar with the tools available to determine people's preferred team roles and it is suggested that great benefit can be derived by conducting an audit to determine people's preferences about the way they work. The work of Belbin (1993) is seminal in this field.

4.6.6 Performance management – is there a system in place to provide performance management for support staff?

The lack of a performance management system was not listed among the highest concerns by the MMU SBM group, but there were gaps in provision and a lack of a nationwide performance management system on a par with that for teachers and headteachers was identified. If a national system for performance management of support staff were to be instituted in line with nationally agreed competencies for the various roles, then this would be a major step forward in the improvement of support staff management. In the meantime the school may do well in determining a school-based system to meet the specific needs of a school and its deployment of staff if there is no such system in place. How SBMs could implement such a system, applying quality management principles, would be the subject of further debate and writing.

However it is worth mentioning that reviewing performance with stakeholders offers an opportunity to align personal career targets with school targets, thus ensuring that resources spent on staff training and development are consistent with school priorities.

4.6.7 CPD – is it offered to teaching assistants? Is there consistency and equal opportunity? Is it matched to the needs of the school and the needs of the TA? Is it matched to teaching and learning outcomes and can these be measured?

It may be that not all of these questions are answerable in the short term, but the whole area raises a useful line of enquiry as to what is happening in terms of professional development. This in turn is linked to motivation, morale and retention of staff quite as much as it is related to the improvement of support in the classroom. Most of the MMU SBMs reported a low turnover of TA staff, stating frequently that the reason that TAs stayed in their posts was explained more by domestic reasons (the conditions of the job, the suitability of the hours and the friendliness of the school) than the notion of quality of service being provided and career prospects. On the other hand, those SBMs who reported a higher turnover of staff commented that it was due to training opportunities offered by the school and that TA staff looked to develop their careers and apply for degree courses for QTS, for example. So the picture is complicated and neither situation would appear to be cost-effective; on the one hand may be TA staff who are comfortable in stable roles with few career development aspirations, but who may find change difficult, and on the other hand may be TA staff who are eager for training which is supplied by the school, but who then leave to advance their careers.

What you should expect from your TA

I would rather turn this statement on its head, and say that, to secure a highly effective TA, despite the uncertainty of the role, the manager should ask themselves the questions in the box below. If most (six or seven) answers are positive, (s)he will then be providing a workplace context in which it is reasonable to expect high standards of behaviour and attitude from the TA – *who has now been trained and managed appropriately.*

If five or less, then you are not ready, nor in the right context, for the formal supervision of TAs.

	Yes	No
Are you involved in all the stages of recruitment in your school? (Particularly with regard to TAs?)		
Are you involved in implementing and monitoring the induction process?		
Are you a trained mentor?		
Can you conduct a skills audit and needs analysis?		
Can you manage a team effectively?		
Are you involved in performance management?		
Are you involved in CPD (organization and implementation) for others in your school?		

4.7 Summary

The recent expansion in the numbers of TAs employed in schools offers potential for school improvement through targeted support of teaching and learning where it is most needed. However it also offers the potential for a certain degree of chaos, if the systems for recruitment and deployment are not managed effectively. Getting the right people is part of the answer to the problem, and the process for recruitment, induction and retention is a system that demands robust and rigorous procedures to secure the right people in the available posts. But as we have seen, that is not the end of the story. If people do not fully understand their roles and responsibilities, feel that they have low status and know that they are poorly paid, then they are unlikely to be giving of their best. Managers find themselves overwhelmed with operational issues as our focus group confirmed. Therefore truly effective deployment becomes nothing other than an unfulfilled aim until the human resource challenges have been addressed. This chapter has sought to describe the landscape of these challenges, using a matrix with which to categorize the issues and identify their strategic importance.

SBMs have the potential to make an impact in the strategic development of the school in two ways: first through recommending and managing a deployment system for TAs and secondly by managing professional/paraprofessional/multi-professional teams. The introduction of RAISE online has resulted in more standardized schools data which is available for school managers to access. Using such data should enable the SBM to highlight trends of achievement in the school and provide timely reports and recommendations for the flexible deployment of teaching assistants in conjunction with consultation with teaching staff and senior leaders. As the boundaries between stakeholders evolve and reform and leadership is increasingly distributed in the flatter hierarchies of twenty-first century schools, so the need for better teamworking increases. SBMs can play a significant role in both these areas and further research will be needed to determine the success or failure of this model.

References

Balshaw, M. and Farrell, P. (2002), *Teaching Assistants: Practical Strategies for Effective Classroom Support*. London: David Fulton Publishers.

BBC (2005), 'Teaching assistants 'exploited', *BBC News,* http://news.bbc.co.uk/go/pr/fr/-/1/hi/education/4316796.stm (accessed 24 May 2007).

BBC (2007), 'Pay frame plan for school staff', *BBC News,* http://news.bbc.co.uk/1/hi/education/6687245.stm (accessed 24 May 2007).

Belbin, M. (1993), *Team Roles at Work*. London: Butterworth-Heinemann.

Bennett, N., Wise, C., Woods, P. and Harvey, J. (2003), *Distributed Leadership*. Nottingham: National College for School Leadership.

Campbell, A. (2005). 'Developing successful practice with support staff' in A. Campbell and Fairbairn, D. (eds) (2005) *Working with support in the classroom*. London: Paul Chapman Publishing.

Campbell, A. and Fairbairn, D. (eds) (2005), *Working with Support in the Classroom*. London: Paul Chapman Publishing.

Chartered Institute of Personnel and Development (2007), *Induction*, www.cipd.co.uk/subjects/recruitmen/induction/induction.htm (accessed 24 May 2007).

Covey, S. (1989), *The Seven Habits of Highly Effective People*. New York: Simon & Schuster.

DfES (2000), *Supporting Teaching Assistants: A Good Practice Guide*. London: DfES.

DfES (2005), *The Effective Management of Teaching Assistants to Improve Standards in Literacy and Mathematics (The Primary National Strategy)*. London: HMSO.

DfES (2006a), *Safeguarding Children and Safer Recruitment in Education*. Nottingham: DfES.

DfES (2006b), *School Workforce in England (including pupil:teacher ratios and pupil:adult ratios), January 2006 (provisional)(National Statistics)*, Nottingham: DfES.

DfES (2006c), *The Deployment and Impact of Support Staff in Schools*. Nottingham: DfES.

Hammett, N. and Burton, N. (2005), 'Motivation, stress and learning support assistants: An examination of staff perceptions at a rural secondary school', *School Leadership and Management*, 25, (3), 299–310.

HMGovernment (2007), *Every Child Matters: Change for Children*, www.everychildmatters. gov.uk (accessed 26 April 2007).

HMGovernment (2007), *Children's Workforce Strategy Update – Spring 2007: Building a World-Class Workforce for Children, Young People and Families.* Nottingham: DfES.

HMI (2002), *Teaching Assistants in Primary Schools: An Evaluation of the Quality and Impact of Their Work*, a report by HMI, www.ofsted.gov.uk/assets/7.pdf (accessed 30 May 2007).

Howes, J. and Murch, I. (2005), 'Should we finance more TAs?' (online) *Times Educational Supplement*, www.tes.co.uk//article.aspx?storycode=2122772 (accessed 12 August 2005).

Hummel, C. E. (1967), *Tyranny of the urgent.* Downers Grove, Il: Intervarsity Press.

Johnson, S., Garland, P. and Coldron, J. (2004), *A Systematic Mapping Exercise to Show How Existing Qualifications Fit with the Proposed Career Progression Framework for School Support Staff.* London: DfES.

Kay, J. (2005), *Teaching Assistant's Handbook: Primary Edition.* London: Continuum.

Keating, I. and Moorcroft, R. (2006), *Managing the Business of Schools.* London: Sage Publications.

Lacey, K. (1999), *Making Mentoring Happen: A Simple and Effective Guide to Implementing a Successful Mentoring Program.* Warriewood, NSW: Business and Professional Publishing.

Matthews, P. (2003), Academic mentoring. *Educational Management Administration and Leadership.* Vol 31. No 3 pp 313–34.

O'Brien, T. and Garner, P. (eds) (2001), *Untold Stories: Learning Support Assistants and their Work.* Stoke-on-Trent: Trentham Books.

O'Leary, D. and Craig, J. (2007), *System Leadership: Lessons from the Literature.* Nottingham: NCSL, www.ncsl.org.uk/media/470/22/system-leadership.pdf (accessed 30 May 2007).

O'Sullivan, F. *et al.* (1999), *From Bursar to School Business Manager: Re-engineering leadership for Resource Management.* London: Pearson Education Limited.

Ofsted (2004), *Remodelling the School Workforce: Phase 1*, www.ofsted.gov.uk/assets/3761. pdf (accessed 25 May 2007).

Ofsted (2005), *Remodelling the School Workforce: A Report from Ofsted*, www.ofsted.gov.uk/ assets/4115.pdf (accessed 25 May 2007).

Reece, B. and Brandt, R. (1993), *Effective Human Relations.* Florence, Kentucky: Cengage publications.

Schön, D. (1991), *The Reflective Practitioner: How Professionals Think in Action.* London: Arena.

Teachernet (2007), *School Workforce: Local Authority Toolkit*, www.teachernet.gov.uk/ docbank/index.cfm?id=11472 (accessed 26 April 2007).

Teaching-Assistants.co.uk (2007), *National remodelling team: Case study*, www.teaching-assistants.co.uk (accessed 26 April 2007).

TDA (2006a), *Developing People to Support Learning: A Strategy for the Wider School Workforce 2006–2009*. London: Training and Development Agency for Schools.

TDA (2006b), *Primary Induction: Role and Context – For Teaching Assistant Trainers*. London: Training and Development Agency for Schools.

TDA (2006c), *Support Staff Induction: Pre-Course Information for Headteacher, Support Staff and their Line Managers*. London: Training and Development Agency for Schools.

TDA (2006d), *Support Staff Induction: Support Staff File*. London: Training and Development Agency for Schools.

TDA (2006e), *The Status of Teachers and the Teaching Profession in England: Views from Inside and Outside the Profession*. London: Training and Development Agency for Schools.

TDA (2008), www.tda.gov.uk/support.aspx.

TES (2007), 'Support staff to get own pay structure', *TES*, 29 May 2007.

TTA (2005), *Building the School Team*. London: Teacher Training Agency.

Vincett, K., Cremin, H. and Thomas, G. (2005), *Teachers and Assistants Working Together*. Maidenhead: Open University Press.

Watkinson, A. (2002), *Assisting Learning and Supporting Teaching: A Practical Guide for the Teaching Assistant in the Classroom*. London: David Fulton Publishers.

Watkinson, A. (2003), *Managing Teaching Assistants: A Guide for Headteachers, Managers and Teachers*. London: RoutledgeFalmer.

Wilson, V., Schlapp, U. and Davidson, J. (2002), *Evaluation of the Classroom Assistants Initiative*, SCRE, www.scre.ac.uk/resreport/pdf/111.pdf (accessed 26 April 2007).

Wood, L., O'Sullivan, F., Rix, S. and Scott, D. (2007), *School Business Managers: Baseline Study Report*. Nottingham: NCSL.

Midday Supervisors   5
Val Butcher

Chapter Outline

5.1 Introduction

This chapter considers some of the issues facing both school and managerial teams concerning supervision taking place during *non-contact* time: before and after the school day; morning and afternoon breaks and at midday. It draws on examples and expertise currently found within the FE sector because, since 2002, it has been possible for 14 and 15 year-old school pupils studying in English schools to follow a vocational programme (Increased Flexibility: IF) in colleges of further education. The initiative offers both benefits and challenges for those involved in the supervision of *younger* students operating in what was traditionally considered to be a post-16 environment. As this development is high profile, the focus of research and management thinking in the area has been intensified. Therefore the chapter will also be applicable to schools – especially secondary schools – as it contains current thinking about an established area of activity which may merit specific attention.

5.2 The legal context

FE colleges adopted the business model following incorporation in 1992. This shift in process management brought about not only a cultural change in terms of working practices, but also a change in personal understanding of the concept of role within the institution. Employees needed to rethink their understanding of the aim and purpose of education and to 'match' it to the new business world they would inhabit. A prime thrust of the new thinking was that *all employees* need to be involved with 'customers' or 'clients' (students) – not just the professional teaching staff.

This new world also reflected perceived national needs, defined as the need to:

- increase participation rates post-16
- produce skilled employees, able to contribute to the national economy
- enable students to become citizens, able to involve themselves in local and wider community issues

This ideology underpinned the activities operating within FE colleges post-2000.

The new business world also brought with it an increase in employees concerned with administration, marketing, and the guidance and support areas of colleges. This is because the national skills agenda was gathering momentum and colleges needed to provide themselves with an array of staff capable of servicing the needs of both the individual client and the organization. Colleges also needed to appoint staff capable of managing *younger* learners – school pupils, aged between 14 and 16 following the introduction of the 'Increased Flexibility' (IF) programme, usually for one morning or afternoon a week.

Colleges choosing to partake in this particular programme continue to wrestle with many challenges – the most significant of which is linked to the *common law duty of care.* In this respect, schools and colleges are subject to the same statutory frameworks, with only the element of the Gillick Principle* differentiating them. Thus for example, both institutions have

---

* Basically, the older a child is (i.e. nearer to 18) the more self-responsibility (s)he is deemed to have.

a common law duty of care to 'enable the parents/carers of young people to have confidence in the institution'. In a context historically populated by older and adult students, the arrival of 14–15 year olds promoted wide-ranging discussions. At the heart of the debate was the care of *children*: defined as 'a person under the age of 18'. Management teams had the delicate task of devising policies which catered for younger learners while maintaining the type of provision attractive to an adult market. Child protection issues and the 'Every Child Matters' agenda led teams to consider practical concerns relating to risk assessment and health and safety matters – while retaining a commitment to an inclusive agenda, offering access to learning for *all* students.

The DfES produced a document entitled: 'Work-related Learning at Key Stage 4' (DfES, 2004); the advice contained within it, however, is not definitive and does not offer '*legal authoritative interpretation*'.

Therefore it is sensible to say that, in answer to the question regarding duty of care, the duty lies in the first instance with the school. The notion of *in loco parentis* is an important one. The pupils belong to the school and it is up to the school to ensure that the placement is a suitable one. Equally, colleges have a responsibility for the health and safety of those on their premises – hence school pupils would come under this remit when *not* involved in lessons. There is obviously a message here for school leadership and management teams – it's up to you to specify what you want from colleges in order to satisfy statutory requirements.

Of note, a more specific role – that of the Learning Support Assistant (LSA) – has a greater 'history' within colleges and schools. Midday supervision for students with particular learning needs would be provided by such personnel. *However, the issue of support for children with learning needs arriving from schools has yet to be resolved at the time of writing.*

5.3 What actually happened?

Let's take an actual example: when Nether College (a pseudonym) chose to open its doors, in 2003, to five hundred 14–15 year olds, the question of responsibility for the children *in between* lessons – 'non-contact' times – quickly arose. Who was responsible for the child on arrival at 9.00? Midday? At the end of the day? The senior leadership team knew that some colleges had devised a rota among teaching staff; others faced negotiations with trade unions before establishing roles and responsibility. Nether College had started to establish good college-schools links *prior* to the arrival of the pupils following the increased flexibility programme – hence the impact was partially reduced, but what should Nether College do?

When considering the nature of the supervision during non-contact time, it became apparent to the management team that a variety of staff would be needed to manage a growing number of students. It also became apparent that the role of the 'midday assistant' was not as clearly defined (or as obvious a role) in colleges as it was in schools. The reason for this can be attributed in part to the nature and ethos of FE. Students who attend college classes (regarded as an adult *environment*) are viewed as 'adults' and as such, requiring little – or less explicit – supervision. To reflect current legislation regarding child protection issues however, it was implicit within managerial philosophy and practice that *younger* learners (children) *would* need to be supervised during the lunch break. The responsibility for the *role* of 'midday supervisor or assistant' therefore was divided between the following personnel:

- head of school
- 14–16 schools – College Link Coordinator
- Student Guidance and Support Manager

These three roles encompassed the notion of care with attached responsibilities linked to behaviour management, and the three held joint responsibility as a team. The advantage of this approach is that there is more comprehensive 'cover' in terms of understanding and decision making. It is the first example of 'good practice': others gained from the research and process implementation are set out below.

5.4 Examples of good practice

To ensure further progress, the following developments took place in Nether College: these have been selected as developments which have transferability and are, in my view, essential for *any* school or college.

- The post of *Schools Link Coordinator* was established. With regard to partnership, the aim was to promote communication links between colleges and schools. However, for schools and colleges *not* working in partnership, the role is useful for monitoring the processes involved within the provision.
- A *policy statement* was devised, outlining the philosophy underpinning supervision of students during breaks and before-and-after school.

- *A School-College Handbook* was devised – setting out rules and responsibilities for all those involved in the IF programme. One version was provided for the school pupils; another for the parents.
- *Lunchtime* hours were *extended and staged* – so that suitably trained staff could be involved with the target group.
- *A nationally accredited course* for midday assistants was delivered.
- *A Student Awards Scheme* centred around achievement and citizenship was introduced – with a specific element of understanding of age issues introduced.

5.5 Key issues

The problems and areas of contention were identified as follows, with one overarching, general 'issue' and several specific elements which need to be considered.

5.5.1 General

There is an implicit difficulty within the notion of supervision of care during non-contact times: how do schools and colleges develop a strategy which ensures that children are able to construct relationships within a community which is not reduced to:

> . . . a very conservative form of schooling . . . surveillance and control, a time and motion like attention to on-work/off-work activities . . .
>
> (Schostak, 1999)

The tension here is obvious. Schostak lifts his argument further by referring to 'an engineering of attention and behaviour to fit demands that come from the powers of industry, government law and order'.

School and college policies do have to 'fit' wider agenda but creativity and ingenuity should not be forsaken while attempting to do so. The role of the senior leadership/management/business team (and arguably, specifically the school business manager) includes the ability to draw on the demands of existing legislation and yet interpret the requirements in such a way that the child is 'free' to learn while engaged in both contact and non-contact activities. If not, we may have the option of following the route chosen by Alan McMurdo, the chief executive of a new 'super school' in Cambridgeshire.

Mr McMurdo has chosen to abolish playtime and to reject the building of a school playground, offering the view that it is time to end the 'tyranny that playtime exercised over the traditional school day'. The notion of 'improved productivity' appears to be at the centre of the debate but it can also be suggested that such a debate exposes the tensions existing in the practice of education-as-a-business vs that of, for example, healthy working practices and well-being.

5.5.2 Specific

The issues are pertinent for all colleges and most apply to schools. They include:

- *the need for appropriate training of all staff at all levels*. Fourteen year olds are *children* and bring with them learning experiences and stages of maturation not previously managed within the FE environment or necessarily known to adults who may only have knowledge or experience with much younger children. HR departments in colleges need to be actively involved with the needs of academic and business support staff in order to support the holistic approach to learning and to provide a related, structured, staff development programme. In schools, this task should be vested in the school business manager.
- *the importance of internal and external planning.* Working with school pupils requires a shared understanding of expectations and a communication of such an understanding to all stakeholders. To establish and develop links between schools, learners, parents and colleges requires leadership and commitment which is not short term. In a post-16 environment this is exacerbated by different contexts of personal responsibility. Again, the school business manager is well placed to deal with this aspect, usually having a background in industry/commerce and a role less dedicated to actual learning and teaching.
- *knowledge and implementation (as opposed to awareness) of the requirements surrounding the issues of duty of care.* One of the greatest concerns with this age group is the likelihood of accidents – especially during non-contact times. The midday supervisor needs to have knowledge of the accident reporting system and protocols and procedures surrounding this. The school must always be informed of any accidents occurring while on college placements, and the school may have its own procedures which need to be followed in order to completely fulfil the duty of care. Clearly this is an administrative function which falls into the remit of the school business manager.
- *younger learners needing to learn 'new' rules.* The college environment is unfamiliar and school pupils may feel unsettled for a while. Coming from a school context, their views on the workings of the FE environment may be based on

assumptions – often drawn from the media. Many arrive with the view that they will be allowed to 'mimic' adult behaviour and to operate in a world where 'rules don't exist'. The supervisor involved in this role needs to understand and communicate that the safety of the young person remains paramount and underpins all activities surrounding the learner. This is often difficult for staff who may have, for example, different views regarding pupil behaviour. Again, the school business manager is ideally placed to influence students: as a non-teacher, the peculiarities of the workplace can be better communicated by a real-life 'worker'!

- *providing a profile of the school pupil.* Such a profile needs to offer concordance with the Data Protection Act and to embody notions of confidentiality. It should also provide information designed to enhance the caring provision for those supervising the younger learner. This information needs to be controlled, and the answer to one best practice question, 'Will telling the supervisor this (information) help her/him to help the child?' is usually 'no!' Do I need to say that this is absolutely the domain of the school business manager?

5.6 What you should expect from your midday supervisor

As a manager of the school or college, you should reasonably expect midday and other types of non-contact care to demonstrate a clear knowledge and understanding of three key elements:

1. *Their role within the provision* – clearly explained and defined within pro forma such as role or job descriptions. You should also expect *some* knowledge and understanding of their role as contained within other, specific school policy documents, for example the School Mission Statement – especially where there is 'block attendance' from one school.
2. *Health and safety issues,* protocols and procedures and, most importantly, their role within the statutory framework.
3. *Their need to engage with internal and external training* events offering an update on current legislation pertaining to care of the child, and more specifically, awareness of the educational objectives attached to their role – even if only to 'enable the parents/carers to have confidence in the institution'.

The above list implies that is no longer possible for midday or other supervisory staff to 'turn up' at the prescribed hour without a wider awareness of their role. While accepting that pay rates may not always reflect the role, it is necessary to also accept that client and stakeholder perceptions and enactment of the role have changed in accordance with wider issues relating to, for example, child protection or learning methodologies.

5.7 Strategies to adopt to maximize usefulness of role

So, how to do this? How to ensure successful implementation of, for example, the IF programme? It has been noted above that the SBM has a significant role to play in ensuring the smooth running of such a provision (operational perspective) but more importantly, they can be *instrumental* in establishing or devising policy and practice (strategic perspective). (S)he could consider five areas of activity:

1. Making links with internal and external personnel:
   - *External links* include working with the college Student Guidance Manager and/ or the Schools Link Coordinator. The majority of colleges operate a student guidance/support network and the person occupying either of these roles is likely to be involved in caring for the younger learner.

      Understanding the role of the Learning Support Assistant (LSA) is equally important. The role has strong curriculum links and is designed to enhance the process of teaching and learning. The LSA can offer an additional perspective on learner needs and although noted here in the college context, there is no reason why the ideology cannot be shared or transferred to school-based philosophies (refer to the chapter by Coulbeck in this book).

      Working with *other* partners or community organizations – such as *Business Link* – will provide additional support and further the aim of offering an integrated approach to work-based learning.
   - *Internal links* include *working with staff* involved in the nomination of appropriate pupils for the college-based programme. This would involve the development of criteria which could be shared with other stakeholders and which would form part of existing documentation.
2. Ensuring clear communication between college and school governing bodies to ensure that issues linked to off-site provision are explicit.
3. Developing a policy for college-based, work-related learning that is consistent with *other* school policies, for example one that covers inclusion, equal opportunities, careers education and guidance.
4. Implementing placement risk assessments, health and safety checks, as appropriate and in line with current legislation. Coupled with this is the need to review current insurance policies and to take professional advice where necessary.
5. Communicating personnel issues to staff via the staff development network, for example requirements pertaining to CRB checks; rules regarding children studying in classes occupied by over-18s.

5.8 Summary

The SBT is in 'pole position' regarding supervision of care during non-contact time – it is their responsibility. A strong argument for making this part of the school business manager's role has been made here. He or she can lead change in what is regarded as a fairly new (certainly in colleges) area of operations – but one which should be a continuing part of the curriculum. The role involves more than that of facilitator; it involves a strong awareness of current legislation matched to an ability to implement and communicate related strategies across school and college mechanisms – while accommodating the stated visions of both.

In conclusion, while acknowledging that the issue of care gives rise to practical concerns, it is also fair to say that supervision during non-contact time is connected with three wider issues:

- *Student entitlement* – providing supervision which acknowledges personal freedom and manages abuse of such freedoms.
- *Citizenship* – providing an environment which allows pupils the opportunity to develop the personal and social skills needed to 'grow' as an individual operating within a larger community and society.
- The advancement of *education in its widest sense* as opposed to 'schooling' the child.

References

DfES (2003), *Work Related Learning at Key Stage 4*. London: DfES.

DfES (2004), *Every Child Matters*. London: DfES.

McMurdo, A. quoted in *The Times*, May 2007.

Qualifications Curriculum Agency, www.qca.org.uk/14-19/index.html.

Schostak, J. F. (1999), 'Action research and the point instant of change', *Educational Action Research*, 7, 3.

Further reading

Gray, P., Miller, A. and Noakes, J. (1994), *Challenging Behaviour in Schools: Teacher Support, Practical Techniques*. London: Routledge.

Jackson, C. and Bedford, D. (2005), 'Unlocking the potential: The enhanced role of support staff for schools in England', paper presented at the International Congress of School Effectiveness and Improvement, Barcelona, 3 January 2005.

Useful websites

www.skills4schools.co.uk/page.asp?id=235: This site provides a brief overview of the roles and responsibilities of midday supervisors.

www.teachingexpertise.com/articles/transforming-lunchtimes-666: An excellent site which provides much practical advice on the effective deployment of midday supervisors, with suggestions on behaviour management strategies and how to engage with children at lunchtimes.

Part Three
The External Professionals

Business Partnerships

Paul Matthews

6

6.1 Introduction

I'm a businessman, so this chapter is about my perspective on building a relationship with business. In my business life, I have always found that long-term arrangements are much more satisfying for both parties than a short 'affair'! Therefore I'll start by saying that the process of building the relationship needs care and planning to move from initial courtship into a mutually beneficial long-term partnership. Take a look at the typical scenario set out in the box below.

Example: On the spot . . .

You are a member of the school business team and the chair of governors says to you one day: 'Why is the school down the road always in the press and on the local radio about the really innovative activities they augment their curriculum with?'

Then the headteacher in a bi-monthly planning meeting talks about finding out how the school can work with local businesses to get some real partnerships going. She thinks there must be benefits to both the students and staff alike from building such relationships.

Sounds familiar?

So where to start? What steps do you need to take first? How can you make it all come together and work?

6.2 Legal requirements and other paperwork

Please note that this chapter does not offer formal legal advice as each situation will vary. Please make sure you do get formal advice if you are at all worried, the local authority should be able to help you here. There is, however, a curriculum imperative, which is arguably a 'legal' requirement. This revolves around the ECM Agenda – specifically, the 'achieve economic well-being' strand.

Stakeholders in the school will certainly want to be assured that nothing illegal is happening in setting up a business partnership. However, being pragmatic about it, it is unlikely that you will need any formal legal documents, in fact unless there is a significant amount of money involved it is probably best not to have a contract. What you really want is to develop a relationship based on trust and mutual benefit. After all a contract is only really a document that is used to hold each of the parties involved to account if something goes wrong with a transaction or project delivery.

A good way of having something that formalizes the relationship a little can be a partnership agreement or 'Memorandum of Understanding' (MOU) which both the school and the business can sign.

These agreements should not be seen as legal documents but will add a degree of formality. Areas to cover in such a document could be as follows:

- to work in partnership for a given time period
- to share ideas and support each other
- to promote the relationship in the media where appropriate
- to give equal prominence in any promotions and projects that are run
- joint sign – off of statements which promote the relationship
- agreement to review the relationship on an annual basis

If appropriate, and depending on your school status, you might also have local authority guidance on third party involvement in schools so it is certainly a good idea to check with them as well.

6.3 What do you bring to the party?

What business will expect to see is a document that identifies the benefits they can expect from the relationship. Knowing what your school can bring to the relationship is therefore important.

Think outside the box a little on this one. Your school will be a centre of excellence for teaching and learning and a range of other skills local business might like to develop. Perhaps local business might want their training departments to tap into that teaching expertise.

What's our offering?

Action point: Get a group of teaching and non-teaching staff together and work out what benefits your school can bring to any relationship. A SWOT analysis might be a good first step. Write these benefits up as a leaflet that you can give to any business as a summary of very good reasons why you should be working together.

During the relationship a business will expect to see some formal documents like meeting agendas, meeting notes (send those notes if you can within three working days of a meeting), service level agreements if necessary and certainly invoices if money is to change hands at all (please remember the new FMSiS rules here). Using these types of documents will show a high degree of professionalism on your part which will only enhance the relationship further as you move forward.

Please remember if you are exchanging personal data you need to check the data protection regulations. These are all on the Information Commissioner's Office website (www.ico.gov.uk) and the local authority will also be a good source of information.

Another point to remember is that business will probably not know the need for people involved with vulnerable groups to undergo CRB checks. So if your relationship involves business people coming into school and interacting with students it's probably best to tell them about these requirements up front.

Don't be put off by the legal issues; any regulations are there for protection but (and it may not seem like that) are intended *not* to get in the way of enhancing the school and its environment by a well-considered and developed outreach programme.

6.4 Choosing the right business

Perhaps the most important aspect of developing a relationship is choosing the right partner.

Here's a six step plan to making sure you do choose the right one and have the rest of the school on your side as well. The six points are summarized in the box that follows these steps.

1. Step 1 – Make sure the concept of developing links with local business is written into the school development strategy and that the key stakeholders support you. This way, if you need resources as you progress, you are more likely to get them. Talk it through with the headteacher to start with and get their view. In the example above it was the headteacher and chair of governors who raised the concept of business relationships but just think how much more powerful it would have been if you had raised it first.

2. Step 2 – Identify all the projects in school that would benefit from a business involvement. For example, you might want to redesign or even launch your school website or you might have obtained funding to develop an area of the school into an environmental area. It might be that business has skills you want your staff to take advantage of. There is a good example of this type of partnership set out in the list of activities towards the end of this chapter that a community primary school based in Prescot, Merseyside has undertaken as part of its business partnership activity.

    Remember businesses have a wealth of skills and experience that they will more than likely be happy to share with you if they have time. A note of caution however: asking for funding in the first instance is what they will probably expect you to do and so asking for their time might well come as a pleasant surprise. Once the relationship is established and working, then money can be put on the table if that is an objective.

3. Step 3 – List the skills needed to deliver the projects. Each project is likely to need a specific set of skills so just list them. For the examples in Step 2 this might be web design skills or environmental awareness.

4. Step 4 – Identify businesses that have these skills. Conduct some research into local business to see which ones are likely to have the skills you need. So, do they have a really good website or do you know they have a design team or environmental awareness awards?

5. Step 5 – Ask parents and suppliers if they know the business. The next step is to see if you already know someone who knows the business you are trying to form the relationship with. Ask your parents and suppliers if they know them and if not then ask the local chamber of commerce if they are members. Try and get the name and title of a senior person in the business who can make a decision on supporting your school.

Build a network

Action point: Good communication is really important if a business partnership is going to work well. Tell your parents via a special assembly or a note home of your plans and reinforce the point that their children will potentially benefit from the activities the relationship is designed to generate. Send a questionnaire home so you know where parents work and update this every two years.

6. Step 6 – Draw up a short list of businesses you know that you have contact with and who have the skills you need. Don't choose too many as you will not be able to successfully manage the relationship if you have too many partners.

Example: Choosing well

1. write into your SDP, 'developing business links'
2. audit your school for potential projects
3. identify the skills required
4. identify the businesses with these skills
5. who do you know who knows someone in the business?
6. pick the best!

6.5 Getting in contact

You will now be ready to take the next step in the process, which is making contact with your proposed business partner.

This is perhaps the most critical stage in the relationship as first impressions count and so planning time spent here will be time well spent.

The first contact should be by telephone followed up with a well-written letter, addressed to the individual you talked to and signed by the headteacher.

Contact by telephone sounds simple and straightforward but as you will not be having a face-to-face conversation it is also very easy for the person at the other end of the telephone to object to what you are asking for.

A simple technique is to think in advance of the objections you might well have to deal with during that initial call and draft some answers to those comments. Then role play the call a couple of times before you make it.

Here are a few examples of the types of objection you might come across but work some out for yourself as well and script some answers:

- we don't sponsor anyone here
- I am sorry but we have already spent our budget for this type of activity
- we would really like to help but we are too busy at the moment
- the person you need to speak to is away at the moment
- we already support a local school

A plan for that initial telephone call might look like the one set out in the box below.

Example: The first call

- Explain who you are and your role in the school.
- Thank them for taking the call.
- Explain that schools are an important centre of the community and you want to involve all the community in school life, which is why you are contacting them.
- Explain the concept of a business partnership – emphasize here that it is not just about funding but skills transfer.
- Explain the benefits to the business from an involvement. Use the leaflet you will have designed from the first action point in this chapter as a prompt.
- Seek and confirm their support.

- Offer to put it in writing.
- Offer them a visit to the school to discuss the matter further and if they are in agreement offer to send an agenda, map of the school etc.
- Thank them again and finish the call.

Follow up the call that day with a letter that confirms the date and time of the first meeting, posted 1st class; 2nd class sends the wrong message – if it gets there! Include the benefits leaflet you will have drafted from the first action point in this chapter. Don't forget to thank the business for their interest and set the scene by saying you are looking forward to a long and mutually beneficial relationship.

6.6 The first meeting

You will by now have at least the basis of a relationship with a local business and the first meeting will help you to cement that relationship and make it real. There are three 'big requirements' for this first meeting:

1. Don't try and cover too much ground.
2. If at all possible arrange for it to take place at school. This gives you a good opportunity to use the students to impress the business and gain their commitment to supporting you.
3. Don't use jargon! ('ECM' may be meat and drink to you, but may sound like medicine to a business person)

OK, that's the 'big picture', but what about the details? Here are some practical tips to ensuring a successful first meeting:

- have a car park space reserved for your visitor and tell them you have done that in advance
- brief the reception area that they are coming in and ask them to make their greeting extra specially welcoming
- let the reception know where you will be in school when your visitors arrive so that they are not kept waiting
- in the agenda you send them beforehand identify who will be at the meeting from school and their role and ask them who will be coming from their end
- offer tea and coffee on arrival

- stick to the agenda and the allocated meeting time
- fit in a tour of the school particularly the area you want them to support you in
- get the students involved if you can, even if it is just a quick hello
- make sure you set a date and time for the next meeting
- at the end of the meeting, personally show them out with a firm handshake and smile, not forgetting to thank them for their time

This may sound like simple common sense but if you are not used to setting up and running this type of meeting it provides useful terms of reference.

A draft agenda for the first meeting might look something like the one set out in the box below.

Example: Agenda for the meeting of XYZ School and ABC Business Limited

Monday 10 May 2008–11 a.m. to 12.30 p.m.

Present:
Mrs A – XYZ school business manager
Mrs B – XYZ school headteacher
Mr C – XYZ Year 6 class teacher
Mrs D – ABC manager
Mr E – ABC supervisor

1. welcome and introductions
2. background to XYZ school
3. background to ABC business
4. the school in the wider community and a supplier of the future workforce
5. overview of the XYZ school project you want to develop with the business including the nature of the support required
6. ABC view on the project
7. roles and responsibilities
8. any other business
9. date of the next meeting
10. tour of the school
11. meeting close – 12.30 p.m

6.7 Maintaining the relationship

Now you have established the relationship and have at least one project to work on, keeping it moving forward will be important and will need your attention and commitment.

First, agree a set of regular meetings to review your progress, perhaps as many as four to six a year in the early years. These meeting dates should be put in the diary well in advance and only cancelled under exceptional circumstance. These meetings will ensure a regular dialogue flows between the school and the business partner and that a forum to discuss ideas for new projects is always available.

It is also well worthwhile having an annual plan of activities which will help self-manage the relationship. Perhaps consider putting it up in the staff-room to keep people involved in the programme. The template offered in the box below will help you to set out a plan that ensures all parties involved know what is happening when and who is responsible for what element. Importantly it also includes a review date for each project. This review will help to ensure the relationship continues to be beneficial to both parties. This is an important point as an honest assessment of the worth of the partnership to both parties, or at least an opportunity to have that open and honest assessment, will help maintain a positive and productive atmosphere between the school and business partner.

Use this plan each meeting to make sure work is on track and the relationship is delivering the mutual benefits both parties sought at the outset.

Example: Template management plan

Project area	Date of commencement	Specific activities	Responsibilities	Date	Review date
Website redesign	5/1/2009	Agree content	School	1/2/2009	
		Produce draft design and copy	Business partner	1/3/2009	
		Sign off design and copy	Both parties	20/3/2009	
		Test site	Business partner	1/4/2009	

Example: Template management plan—Cont'd

Project area	Date of commencement	Specific activities	Responsibilities	Date	Review date
		Brief local press	Both parties	10/4/2009	
		Launch site	Both parties	20/4/2009	2/5/2009
Redesign school prospectus	1/2/2009	Research stakeholders on document content	School	25/2/2009	
		Agree new content	School	5/3/2009	
		Design new prospectus	Business partner	7/4/2009	
		Approve design and text	Both parties	3/5/2009	
		Print	Business partner	20/5/2009	
		Launch new document		1/6/2009	1/7/2009

6.8 Generating publicity

An important area not to forget is publicizing the benefits of the relationship to all those stakeholders who might benefit from knowing about it. One area a business partner might well be interested in is the opportunity to generate good local public relations (PR) by linking to influential local organizations like schools.

Strengthening the network

Action point: Draw up a list of the key internal and external stakeholders you should consider including in your communications. Remember to involve the local media (press, radio, internet sites etc.) as this will widen the audience the information can reach. Use that list every time a project is being planned to make sure all interested parties know about it.

Your local authority will probably have a PR section, or even media handling protocols, so it is well worth having a conversation with them about this important area.

Keep a media book in school with copies of all the times the school and the business partner relationship appears. Have that book available for your regular meetings with your business partner. This will show a tangible benefit from the relationship which can only help strengthen the bond between the two organizations.

Dealing with the media also requires some consideration and so set out below are some basic tips to follow, though it is by no means a comprehensive list:

- Have one person nominated as your media spokesperson and give them some training if necessary.
- Encourage that person to develop a relationship with the media so that when they might need information on a local educational issue your school is the first place they think to contact.
- Keep the media advised well in advance of your plans; this way the project you want to let people know about has a better chance of getting space in the newspaper or on to the radio.
- Consider having one of the key local media as a business partner.
- Read any press releases carefully before they are issued making sure to check website addresses or contact telephone numbers contained in it for accuracy.

6.9 Does it work?

So does establishing business relationships really work for schools?

Set out below are a few examples of projects that one forward thinking primary school, Evelyn Community Primary School in Prescot, Merseyside has managed to implement through a progressive and positive attitude towards forming relationships with local business.

In its last inspection, the school was rated as outstanding in all areas by Ofsted.

6.9.1 Healthy school initiative and promotion of after-school club facilities

The school teamed up with Everton Football Club and the after-school club dance group performed a specially choreographed dance on the pitch before the start of a televised premiership game.

The whole school got behind the initiative and parents were invited by Everton FC to see the dance and attend the match. The local media covered the story and a significant amount of positive publicity was generated. Parents viewed the relationship as positive as it provided their children with a unique opportunity they would not have otherwise been able to take advantage of.

Subsequently a small group of Year 6 students were invited to participate in the national media launch of one of Everton's youth development initiatives. They presented to the national press, television and radio at Goodison Park, Everton's home ground – a unique experience which the students said they would not forget.

6.9.2 Business skills

A local business agreed to come into school and discuss with Year 6 students basic business skills. Students were asked to design their own product idea (these ideas ranged from a school magazine promoting reading and numeracy to a series of confectionery products) and then present a business case to that local business to release funding. The total budget for this initiative was £150 so it need not be expensive. Students then implemented their plans in school and a winning team was chosen by a panel of local business leaders. Students benefited from this activity in a variety of ways including the further developing of their interpersonal skills, problem solving, maths, English and presentation skills as well as deadline and budget management skills. It also gave the students an indication of what working in a business was like. The winning team generated a return on initial investment of over 500 per cent! Prizes for the winners and runners up were provided by a local cinema.

6.9.3 Relaxation techniques to improve student attention in class

The school implemented 'Relax Kids' techniques in class which are designed to help children relax and concentrate in lessons. Evelyn Community Primary School wished to bring the advantages of this activity to the attention of parents. In order to do this it teamed up with a local relaxation and beauty salon with national award winning staff. They offered the parents relaxation treatments while during the same presentation the school informed parents of the benefits of using the Relax Kids techniques. Parents found the session very helpful and commented that the opportunity for them to relax while being informed about the creative way the school was supporting the curriculum was most helpful and impressive.

6.9.4 Environmental awareness

In partnership with the local safari park the school has worked on a number of joint projects.

In particular the park wished to promote the plight of amphibians, some of which are in danger of extinction from a virus sweeping the globe. Students at the school produced a play informing people of the virus and the consequences if action is not taken. This play was filmed and shown at the safari park during one of its educational weeks and over 1,000 visitors saw the play and the link with the school. It went further as the play was subsequently shown at a meeting of major European safari park staff and so the school's name and the quality of its students work now has an international reputation.

6.9.5 Leadership benchmarking

The school has an active continuous professional development programme and wanted to be able to set benchmark standards for leadership and management in a school context. The school again teamed up with a local business that had developed a series of leadership benchmarks. The school used the methodology and guidance of that local business to produce its own staff and governor leadership benchmark criteria. This criteria is now used extensively in a range of HR issues in school including recruitment, CPD development and performance management.

This last example well illustrates that the advantages of business links not only benefit students but also staff if the people responsible take a creative view of what local business can offer.

6.9.6 Teachers TV

As a result of the activities above and a range of other in-school-based initiatives Evelyn Community Primary School was featured on Teachers TV as a centre of excellence for the delivery of a creative and engaging curriculum.

6.10 Summary

Developing relationships with business can be a rewarding and interesting experience.

The simple rules contained in the chapter (many of which are just plain common sense) will help you make sure your business relationships are right for your school and benefit both parties; that is really the key to success.

Managing the relationship does take time and effort but the rewards to both students and staff can be significant.

Above all, however, a carefully chosen relationship can help deliver an enhanced teaching and learning environment in school where the experiences students and staff can take advantage of will benefit them immeasurably in the future. As a member of the school business team what more important contribution could you make to the life of the school this year?

So . . . for better or worse? If properly planned and implemented it has got to be for the better.

Further reading

Tuten, T. and Urban, D. (2001), 'An expanded model of business-to-business partnership formation and success', *Industrial Marketing Management*, 2, 149–64, www.sciencedirect.com/science?_ob=ArticleURL&_udi=B6V69-42BTKST-6&_user=121753&_rdoc=1&_fmt=&_orig=search&_sort=d&view=c&_acct=C000010022&_version=1&_urlVersion=0&_userid=121753&md5=40baa2326572cf1f6a36756696b77d67 (accessed 16 June 2008).

Useful websites

www.nebpn.org/aboutus.htm: The NEBPN is the umbrella organization and national voice for 126 education business partnerships. Its role is to advance the education of pupils and students, at local schools and colleges in particular, by promoting the efficiency of education and business partnerships in England and Wales and Northern Ireland so as to improve the educational preparation and training of young people to prepare for proper employment. A comprehensive website with much useful information for schools considering greater links with local businesses.

The Educational Law Officers
Inspector Saied Mostaghel

7

7.1 Introduction

The concept of policemen as partners in education is not something which sits easily with many teachers. Given a situation where the learning centre is often the only place for some children where the police are not interacting on a daily, oppositional basis, teachers can be reluctant to be perceived as being too close to officers. However, this chapter is based on the premise that effective partnerships can enhance education, and the Safer Schools Partnerships (SSP) programme provides strong evidence for this. The SSP programme has been developed in line with national mainstreaming guidance produced by DCSF, the Youth Justice Board of England and Wales and the ACPO Youth Issues Group. This guidance follows a small number of pathfinder pilots which commenced in 2002: since this time a further 300 pilots of police officers in schools have been conducted across England and Wales. The University of

York, Centre for Criminal Justice and KPMG have evaluated SSP pilots and have produced guidance on best practice.

Findings from this work indicate that SSPs have the ability to significantly impact on crime and antisocial behaviour reduction in and around schools. Reductions in truancy and school exclusions have been achieved in every school involved in the pilot. School attainment levels have increased and relationships between police officers and pupils, and staff and parents have been significantly enhanced. All schools report being safer learning environments as a result of these initiatives.

Such results are worth pursuing, so this chapter focuses on what leadership staff in learning centres need to do in order to secure the benefits for their organization. It describes the attempts of one police authority, Merseyside, to introduce the SSP into its area, and highlights exemplars of good practice along with points to consider carefully in implementing such a scheme.

7.2 The legal context

A police officer has no more right to enter a school than s/he has to enter any private building. The fact that it is connected to a public sector activity is irrelevant.

However, the new powers given to senior staff in respect of, for example, searching pupils (albeit that they are reluctant to take them up) means that senior staff are more likely to invite police into the building as they discover illegal items or activities.

Similarly, police officers have the right to enter learning centres if they have just cause to believe an offence is, or has been, committed. However, more advanced management in the police believe it is more sensible and effective to be more proactive and to change perceptions (on both 'sides') about the role of the police officer with respect to education. The term, 'Educational Law Officer' will be used here to reflect this approach, but as will be seen, it has a wider application. Of course, changing culture is a long-term activity, and hence the research and effort taken with regard to programmes such as SSP.

The sample protocol set out in this chapter provides indicative guidance to key points of concern, such as infractions of the Data Protection Act, but local contexts should always be considered. If both parties are actively engaged in the partnership, then the legal aspects will be overtly discussed and adequately covered.

Case study

It was the ambition of Merseyside police to mainstream Safer Schools Partnerships (SSPs) within Merseyside secondary schools by April 2007. Merseyside has 112 secondary schools across five local authority areas. These secondary schools range from fee-paying private schools to pupil referral units dealing with school exclusions. Police support for schools is identified in collaboration with local authority children's services and headteachers. SSP strategic steering groups have been established in all five Merseyside local authorities with police representation from chief inspectors working within each authority. These steering groups will manage the development and implementation of SSPs based on local needs.

It is clear to all concerned that the police service has a role to play in supporting a safer school environment. It is not, however, appropriate for a police officer to be placed in every school across Merseyside. Contact with schools and the range and scope of activity must be delivered in line with need. At this time, 32 schools have been identified for this scheme; currently police officers are working at 16 schools across Merseyside and it is anticipated this figure will be increased to the target of 32 in the next few months.

Merseyside police have collaborated with partners in relation to analysing data to identify the level of support for each secondary school and feeder primary. This data has been tabled into two categories, social data and crime data. The social data includes four weighted measures: school exclusion, truancy, attainment and index of social deprivation. Crime data includes all crime committed in and against schools and the wider community within 500 metres of the school premises. A hierarchy of data has been produced for use by SSP strategic steering groups to assist the decision-making process on placing police officers in schools in their area. Recommendations on the appropriate level of support have been provided in line with the following contact matrix:

- **Single School Officer** – Officer placed within a single secondary school supporting all feeder primary schools.
- **Cluster Schools Officer** – Officer supporting a cluster of secondary schools supporting all feeder schools.
- **Dedicated Neighbourhood Officer** – Secondary school supported by local Dedicated Neighbourhood Officer and all feeder primary schools.

	Objective	Activity	Success criteria
One	Reduce crime, antisocial behaviour and victimization.	Deliver key messages on local and antisocial behaviour issues.	Reduction in crime within 500 metres of schools. Reduction in calls for service in ASB within 500 metres of school.
		Develop school's intelligence.	Reduction in young people becoming victims.

⇨

Case study—cont'd

	Objective	Activity	Success criteria
		Maximize opportunities for crime reporting and sanction detections.	Increase in sanction detection rate.
Two	Support a safer school environment .	Support pupils through transition. Tackle race and hate crime. Conduct patrol in and outside schools.	Improved perceptions of safety in schools.
		Develop key partnerships including local communities.	Reduction in school-based crime within 500 metres of school.
		Support initiatives on whole-school approach to safety.	Increased confidence and satisfaction from pupils, staff and parents/carers.
Three	Challenge unacceptable behaviour.	Support anti-bullying initiatives. Support schools behaviour contracts.	Improved behaviour. Reduction in school exclusions.
		Utilize restorative justice practices. Challenge discrimination and promote equality.	Reduction in truancy rates.
Four	Support attendance.	Encourage school attendance. Provide support for excluded pupils. Work with young people at high risk of exclusion.	Reduction in school exclusions.
		Support truancy initiatives.	Reduction in truancy rates. Reduction in crime and antisocial behaviour within 500 metres of school.

It is paramount that headteachers and staff work in partnership with police officers and other partners through this process. It is only through a meaningful participation and engagement by all parties that we can make a real difference in promoting a Safer Schools Partnership programme.

7.3 Practical implications for leaders and managers in schools

The first step is to familiarize yourself and everybody in the team with the principles for devising a protocol, which should then be issued jointly by the key stakeholders; a sample is provided below. The protocol itself sets out a framework for interaction covering issues such as when uniforms should be worn in schools through to examples of appropriate information sharing. A sample protocol (for guidance only) is provided at the end of this chapter, but if involved in setting up such a partnership, all parties need to check whether they comply with the principles.

Key principles: Police/school protocols

Introduction
This document is intended to provide a framework for the development of local protocols to establish effective programmes of joint working between schools, local police and partnership agencies. The purpose of the protocol is:

- to help promote dialogue and further develop effective partnerships between schools, police and other agencies that are based on cooperation and shared understandings
- to set expectations for local partnerships, while allowing police services and schools to address service-delivery arrangements and local circumstances
- to define the respective roles and responsibilities for the police, schools and partnership agencies

The key principle in drawing up a protocol should be to enhance the learning environment by providing a safe and secure school community.
It should deliver:

- young people feeling safe and valued
- young people engaged in education, actively learning and achieving at higher levels
- the lowest possible levels of bullying, intimidation and crime experienced by groups of young people

It should not be an end in itself, but a reflection of genuine understanding that enables the involvement of police in schools to be on the basis of regular visible and

Key principles: Police/school protocols—cont'd

well-supported contacts that promote positive outcomes for schools and pupils as well as the police and wider community.

Principles
The following should be considered when drawing up a protocol:

- The need to reflect local circumstances building on successful existing agreements and practice, while taking account of relevant national guidance and legislative requirements.
- Taking account of activities and programmes targeting the social inclusion of young people, both within schools and outside formal education, including Connexions, youth offending teams and any other relevant school/community-based programmes, as well as police, schools and local authorities.
- Links to the school development plan and school support structures.
- Names of those with responsibility for managing the relationships, including:
  a. a senior manager in the school
  b. a police officer as the link with the local police division
  c. an officer of the local authority for each school on crime reduction issues and a senior manager with responsibility for contacts with the police (usually through the crime and disorder partnership)
- The need to record the senior level signatories to the protocol.
- Setting out who has consulted in drawing up the protocol and who will be consulted on changes and informed about activities – including school staff, governors, parents, school councils, students.
- Building in the arrangements for monitoring, evaluation and review of the programme.
- Including the purposes and rationale for the relationship between police and schools; some guiding principles on which the terms of the agreement are based; key objectives linked to outcomes.
- The need to be clear about roles and responsibilities – what the partners to the agreement commit to do, including their formal roles and mandates.
- Setting out the arrangements for information sharing and disclosure in line with the provisions of the Data Protection Act and the Crime and Disorder Act.
- Including the circumstances in which information will be shared, the purpose of the sharing, the types of information that will be shared, who will have access and how access may be obtained, and any commitments about confidentiality. Also, setting out mechanisms for whom to contact in cases of uncertainty about the use of data. (Specific guidance on information sharing will be issued in due course.)

- Stating the provision of resources to be made available by each local authority, school/education establishment and the police in support of this partnership approach.
- Clearly stating and describing the role(s) that police officers will play while in and around the schools, in support of the curriculum, in terms of improving school security as well as staff and pupils' safety and well-being, and in the event of incidents. It should also state the role(s) that schools and local education authority staff will play in and around schools as part of the partnership. It would be advisable to include a process to resolve any misunderstanding or dispute over roles, responsibilities or the provision of resources.

However, there are two ways to implement any protocol: by the book, or with common sense and a commitment to make it work. The second approach is what this chapter is concerned with and is the approach which will ensure an effective and sustainable relationship with your police force. There are five key elements:

1. preliminary meeting(s) – but no more than three – to introduce staff and know the building
2. clarify (at least) the three common occurrences where interaction is likely to occur – including at least one proactive visit
3. ensure common understanding of roles and responsibilities – for example, with regard to lawful search
4. clarify the non-negotiables
5. agree KPIs for evaluating 'success'

Each of these will now be examined in detail, with a particular focus on good practice and innovations, along with tips to make the activity work better for both parties.

7.4 Making it work…

7.4.1 Preliminary meeting(s)

The rationale behind this approach is based on the simple premise that in England, there is one law enforcement officer to 382 people. While the proportions may differ slightly in other countries, the principle remains the same: policing is by the consent and will of the people. It relies on the statistical reality that the majority of people will NOT break the law. It therefore follows that most interactions between the general public and the police take place when the law has been broken, or someone is seriously injured, or there is an emergency of some kind. When the police are involved in a 'good' event, such as the birth of a child in difficult circumstances, it is the stuff of movies, and the media focus on it as an unusual news item.

There are, however, several other issues involved in an educational context which complicate this somewhat simplistic, but pragmatic perspective – not least the long-term approach of both services. For educational professionals, there is the aim of ensuring children voluntarily hold the view that laws exist for the good of themselves and society, and can objectively view those who have the job of enforcing it – whether they agree or not. Without the recognition that 'living for each other entails respect for, and compliance with, laws, whether we like them or not, knowing well that the majority can change them if they wish' (Tacitus), then the teacher's job is impossible – for the principle applies throughout education.

For law enforcement professionals, the same long-term view applies: if they can help children at an early age to recognize that 'the purpose of law is to prevent the strong always having their way' (Ovid), then many of the formative criminal influences, such as bullying, may lose their power – with consequent longer-term implications of a law-abiding society. Therefore both professionals need to recognize that they are both 'educational law officers' (although, in this chapter, the phrase largely refers to the police officer), and the preliminary meetings should be focused on agreeing the general aims of the partnership – remembering that 'aims' are long-term goals, whereas the 'objectives' guide the short-term approach. This may seem somewhat wasteful in terms of time resource, but experience has taught us that to reach an agreed set of values involves extensive and honest debate – which is not something that can be done at the first meeting! Values are private, individual issues, and may take some time to explore, while amendment (compromise) is not to be taken lightly. However, strangely, this approach also fulfils a short-term objective – getting to know the building, which is extremely useful if the school wishes to consult about security, for example.

7.4.2 Common occurrences

Some events in schools are likely to reoccur, such as theft by students, violence in the playground (sadly increasing), antisocial behaviour in the surrounding areas, drugs and so on. However, different schools have different 'commonalities', plus there is also the phenomenon of 'fashionable offences', where offences occur in phases or clusters. Drug abuse is a typical example, when a school is 'targeted' by a dealer. Obviously then, there are two dimensions to the specific approach taken by the partners – each of which can change the priorities – and therefore the situation needs to be monitored. It makes sense to agree a protocol and system which will guide actions in dealing with these particular priorities.

There is however, a tendency to focus on the short-term problems, so good practice involves ensuring that at least one visit should relate to the longer-term educational issues. In other words, an event that isn't reactive, and is part of the broader curriculum (helping fulfil the 'aims').

Take a break . . . Setting priorities

- Set out the analysis of offences and 'issues' which your school suffers from, in *descending* order of occurrence.
  NB: Keep 'offences' separate, as actual convictions in some areas can be low, despite a common understanding that it is a serious issue for the school.
- Engage in discussion with your educational officer about the list – with a specific focus on a priority which can give you a (swift) 'return on investment'.
- Identify one priority which you both agree can only be resolved in the long term.
- Agree the priorities with the SBT and the governing body.

NOTE: What you have done here is to maximize both sets of expertise. Your knowledge of available resources coupled with the officer's experience and knowledge of 'what works' will produce an operational strategy aimed at providing a 'success' – always essential for longer-term, strategic plans to be accepted.

However, be aware: there are strong ethical considerations here . . . a police officer may not have the same freedom of choice as you . . . take a look at the conclusion.

7.4.3 Roles

One way of always ensuring that all staff involved keep a longer-term perspective is to schedule two visits per year which focus on the responsibilities of the educational law officers. One approach we have encountered is that in which each officer talks about the role of the other in fulfilling their responsibilities. Case study: A school (see box below) did this very well, and it again resulted in a clear understanding of the 'boundaries' for all involved.

Case study: A school

An inner-city secondary school had a diverse ethnic student body and a growing problem of racial tension and violence. The school representative used a number of drama sessions to build up a scenario which involved a suspected 'arranged' confrontation between groups of youngsters. It was anticipated that both 'sides' were expected to 'tool up', which meant weapons were to be brought to school. The key question concerned the powers of search.

The police officer became the narrator and led the discussion on the role of the teacher.

7.4.4 Non-negotiables

Some elements of the partnership need to be clarified as non-negotiable. For example, a police officer is never off-duty: awareness of an offence, or the circumstances which can lead to an offence, lays a legal obligation on the officer to do something about it. The same obligation binds the ordinary citizen, but it is almost impossible to enforce, and the educational professional has the ethical dilemma of always placing the child's welfare as a priority. For example, a child often innocently reveals information from a conversation between adults which may involve a potential offence. However, unlike the medical or religious profession, there is no 'sanctity of the classroom'. Nevertheless, understanding of each others' position – and formally setting this out in the protocols – is a sensible approach. When this is done, we have found that both parties prefer to know the boundaries, and are willing to accept the differences. Good practice involves each 'counterpart designated officer' discussing the issue; any reference to a suspected person or problem based on personal knowledge does NOT constitute disclosure under the Data Protection Act.

The whole topic is, of course, also rich and fertile ground for teaching staff to enhance their students' learning about citizenship, and the moral dilemmas of modern life!

7.4.5 KPIs and 'success'

Prior to developments such as the Safer Schools Partnership initiative, evaluating the effectiveness of school–police partnerships was a somewhat vague mechanism. 'Success' was often regarded as a negative: not being ignored, for example! The idea of 'Key Performance Indicators' is to provide *specific* elements against which the project can be judged in terms of a) achievement and b) effectiveness.

Achievement is straightforward: did certain events, such as visits, take place? In the Merseyside initiative, the success criteria were based on accepted 'crime data' elements.

Judging effectiveness of the activities is more complex; for example, how can 'added value' be measured? The answer lies with the school in linking each of the 'accepted' crime data elements to longer-term, education-based aims. For example, one of the criteria in the Merseyside initiative is 'improved behaviour'. The challenge for the school is to analyse exactly what this means, and devise some measures which can be discerned from trend analysis of varied sources of data over a number of years. For example, Ofsted reports on culture of the school, Investors in People evaluations, feedback from anti-bullying initiatives and so on. In other words, producing some discrete measures which apply to the individual school . . . reflecting the belief that working as an educational law officer requires an innovative and creative approach.

7.5 Conclusion

The emphasis on a discrete approach is perhaps the most important practical 'tip' for any member of a school business team. Police officers do not distinguish in terms of 'seriousness' between crimes – contrary to public belief. That is for the criminal justice system to decide. However, when acting in a proactive, advisory role as an educational law officer, (s)he *can* help the school to decide on its priorities – and these *can* vary according to context. The resulting protocols can then be applied much more effectively to a particular school. The key to getting the best out of your officer is perhaps to clarify which 'role' (s)he is undertaking when interacting with him or her – but always to regard it as a positive interaction. This sets expectations which immediately raises the status of the interaction – to a proactive level.

Example: Sample protocol

SAMPLE SAFER SCHOOL PARTNERSHIP PROTOCOL

Joint Protocol

(Name of school/college)

and

Southwark Borough Police

This protocol seeks to clarify the role of the School Beat Officer (SBO) within the school/college and the local community and the working practices for a partnership approach. The aim of this protocol is therefore to ensure that the young people, staff, parents and visitors to the school/college have a safe environment in which to study, work and visit, and where young people can develop to their full potential.

This protocol has been agreed following a consultation process that involved the senior management teams of Southwark Borough Police, the local authority and ----------------- (school/college). (Although unnecessary, Operational Command Units may wish to extend the consultation process to local Independent Advisory Groups and other agencies that have been identified as appropriate for inclusion.) This protocol is a 'live' document that will continue to evolve with the partnership. It will be reviewed formally every 12 months. This review will be conducted by representatives of the borough police and the school and is intended to identify whether the agreement remains current and effective and to identify ways in which it can be improved.

The objectives for the SBO are to:

- continue to improve relations between police and the school/college community, with particular emphasis on the relationship with the pupils
- continue to improve relations between police and the local community
- reduce crime within the school/college beat
- accelerate access to police support at times of need

The partnership objectives are to:

- reduce crime, public disorder and bullying within the school/college beat
- help combat truancy
- reduce the fear of crime among pupils, teachers and other staff, and the wider 'school/college' community
- improve the safety of the school/college beat environment for pupils, teachers, other staff, parents, visitors and neighbours
- support the raising of young people's standard of attainment

Example: Sample protocol—cont'd

- ensure that all members of the partnership follow restorative and problem-solving principles and operate within a multi-agency approach to reduce incidents of crime and antisocial behaviour
- raise the profile of citizenship and the role of individuals and the wider community to achieve it
- provide an environment which improves pupils' motivations and attitudes to learning

The objectives will be achieved through a multi-agency problem-solving panel (MAPS panel) involving representatives from all partners and chaired by a school governor/nominated member of staff.

The role of the SBO is to liaise and negotiate with school/college staff:

- working directly with young people to increase their knowledge of the police service and to develop an effective partnership with the college community
- to adopt both a proactive and reactive response to problem solving in order to reduce crime and disorder within the school community thus improving the environment for young people to learn
- to act as a dedicated investigation liaison officer
- to participate in multi-agency initiatives to improve the school learning environment
- to attend staff, governor and parent meetings as required by their inspector/sergeant

Working practices for partnerships
SBOs in liaison and negotiation with college staff will:

- conduct initial investigations involving allegations of assault (ABH and above), robbery, sexual assault, offensive weapons (knives etc.), possession of class A drugs and possession of drugs with intent to supply
- investigate all other crime reported to police by the school
- assist in a partnership approach to any incidents of bullying and truancy
- assist in a partnership approach to the delivery of the school involvement programme, the educational objectives of which will fit within PSHE and citizenship; other objectives will fit within health action zones and neighbourhood renewal. The areas specific to SBOs are crime; drugs, violence; hate crime; knives/weapons and personal safety.
- undertake school beat patrols
- assist school staff in the management of potentially violent situations
- normally only arrest pupils within school for serious offences. Minor matters will normally be dealt with in other ways after full details have been recorded.
- assist school staff in the lawful searching of pupils

Example: Sample protocol—cont'd

- work in partnership with member of staff so that the SBO may operate in ways which assist staff, where possible, in carrying out their roles effectively
- work with young people to assist them to help deliver a safer and more secure school/college community, and to ensure that their views are actively taken on board in developing the partnership

The following practices also apply:

- Staff will report all incidents of assault (those that result in injury), robbery, sexual assault, offensive weapons seized or found and drugs (as above) to the headteacher who will then liaise with the SBO (third party reporting is acceptable).
- The headteacher will develop an agreement with the SBO on the circumstances in which other crimes are reported to the SBO.
- Staff will assist in a partnership approach to dealing with any incidents including bullying and truancy, and work with the SBO to agree an approach for involving the SBO in its resolution.
- Staff will assist in a partnership approach to the delivery of the schools involvement programme (the education objectives will fit within PSHE, other objectives will fit within Health Action Zones and Neighbourhood Renewal).
- School staff will preserve evidence of an offence whether physical or from a witness whenever practical and will seek the advice of the SBO if required. Continuity of exhibits and property will be given priority. Any exhibits will be brought to the attention of the SBO for them to be dealt with according to service procedures.
- In the event of pupils being searched by school staff police will assist where possible. Staff will conduct searches in the presence of an officer. Parents will be notified of such action by school staff.

Other issues

Uniform

- As a community officer the SBOs will be expected to perform their duties in uniform to enable them to perform their role effectively in support of the school community.
- There will be occasions, however, where it is not practical or desirable for uniform to be worn. Under these circumstances the SBO's line manager may authorize plain clothes to be worn. An example of this may be the case where an SBO is required to speak to a group of people under sensitive

Example: Sample protocol—cont'd

circumstances and it would be detrimental to that process for the police officer to be identified as such to parties not from within this group of people.

Officer Safety Equipment

- All SBOs are required to wear the Officer Safety Equipment. In plain clothes this will be worn covertly using the harness provided. In certain limited situations it may be decided it is not appropriate for the officer to wear their equipment, but in all such situations the equipment must be readily accessible.

Information Exchange

- The exchange of information is covered by the protocol between Southwark police and Southwark Council Local Authority.

7.6 Summary

While the police have some statutory rights with regard to learning centres, in practice the favoured approach is to develop a proactive relationship and to establish 'safer schools partnerships'. Developing close links between individual police officers and a school or cluster of schools allows a more proactive approach to be taken in reducing the incidence of crime and dealing with occurrences. For links to be most effective, they should be underpinned by a clearly thought out and agreed protocol which both parties can subscribe and commit to. Recognize that there are limits – policemen are not teachers, teachers are not policemen. On occasions the requirements of their roles may conflict. If sound protocols are in place the greater the likelihood is that if such instances arise, they can be managed successfully.

Further reading

Jackson, A. (2002), 'Police-school resource officers' and students' perception of the police and offending', *Policing: An International Journal of Police Strategies and Management*, 25, (3), 631–50. Also available at www.emeraldinsight.com/Insight/ViewContentServlet?Filename=Published/EmeraldFullTextArticle/Pdf/1810250309.pdf (accessed 17 June 2008).

DfES (2006), *Safer School Partnerships*. London: HMSO. Also available at www.homeoffice.gov.uk/documents/safer-school-partnerships.pdf?view=Binary (accessed 17 June 2008).

Useful websites

www.met.police.uk/saferschoolpartnerships: This information page, provided by the Metropolitan police force, aims to provide a single point of access to information, resources, contacts and advice for people establishing, developing, operating or working within Safer School Partnership projects. The page is intended predominantly for school-based police officers and teachers, but will be of great value as an information-resource to all personnel and agencies concerned with schools and young people.

www.teachernet.gov.uk/CaseStudies/casestudy.cfm?id=443: A useful case study illustrating the pioneering work done in the Southwark local authority to help improve behaviour by young people.

Facilities Management

Tim Yates

8

8.1 Introduction

The Facilities Manager (FM) at NCSL provides a support role more often found in large commercial organizations where management of the building and services is complex and requires specialized and dedicated management. The exact role and responsibilities of the Facilities Manager (FM) are often numerous in scope, depending very much on the size and complexity of the organization. Many organizations see the FM as being responsible for all support activities that are not part of 'core business' such as catering, cleaning, reception, building and equipment maintenance, grounds maintenance and internal planting; the list is numerous and often growing in nature as support tasks become more complex, regulated and needing specialized management. An FM in a hospital may, for example, be responsible for laundry and sterilization, car parking and retail outlets in addition to catering and cleaning. An FM in a large banking group may be responsible for a portfolio of buildings, a residential training centre and a large computer server room as well as staff facilities. This chapter focuses on the facilities management aspect as it might apply in a school or further education college, and explores two different options for implementation.

8.2 The legal context

The British Institute of Facilities Management (www.bifm.org.uk) define facilities management as *'the integration of processes within an organization to maintain and develop the agreed services which support and improve the effectiveness of its primary activities'*.

What is clear is that the FM will manage a number of vital functions that enable the organization to perform its key tasks in a cost-effective manner, always ensuring that the legal and regulatory requirements of a business are complied with. For example, the FM will ensure that the building is a safe working environment and complies with the Health and Safety at Work Acts, fire regulations and numerous building and maintenance regulations (Legionella testing, pressure vessel testing etc.). They will ensure the food served in the restaurant (as in further education colleges) or food hall complies with the Food Safety Act, the drinks in the bar (for example at parent/teacher events) are served in accordance with the liquor licensing regulations and the staff facilities and workspace complies with the Disability Discrimination Act.

There is a legal requirement for schools and colleges of further and higher education to meet the same building requirements as any commercial business or public facility. Add the daily management of the support services such as school meals, grounds and building maintenance, equipment and asset management, IT service provision and security, and it rapidly becomes apparent that managing these aspects is a full-time and complex task; one that can no longer be completed as part of an additional role for a willing school secretary, janitor or a teacher supported by an enthusiastic board of school governors. The more recent argument is that, where a School Business Manager (SBM) has been appointed, they can 'absorb' the role as part of a wider brief. There is some merit in this approach, as a comparison of a 'standard' job specification for an SBM would resonate with the probable tasks involved, as set out in Table 8.2.1. For the purpose of this chapter, this assumption will be

Table 8.2.1 Facilities management tasks within a school environment

Soft services	Hard services
Catering	Planned preventative maintenance (buildings and plant)
Cleaning	Reactive maintenance
Security/reception	Asset management – plant and equipment, furniture, valuable assets
Vehicle provision	Portable appliance testing
Vending	Health and safety adviser – production of risk assessments and safe systems of work
Reprographics and graphics	Grounds maintenance
Post, courier and internal mail	Window cleaning and specialized 'deep' cleaning
Information technology systems (computer networks, telephony and audio visual equipment)	Building project management
Personal hygiene	Equipment life cycle replacement planning
Marketing of facilities	Energy monitoring
Portering/janitor, furniture moving, relocation	Refurbishments
Special events (weddings, conferences, meetings etc.)	Project management
Science laboratory technical support	Supervision of subcontractors
Procurement – stationery, furniture, equipment, consumables etc.	

made, but it is understood that the role can be adopted by any member of the school business team.

8.3 School business manager as facilities manager

In addition to the service provision the SBM is probably also taking on the role of accountant and budget manager, human resource adviser, strategic business adviser to the headteacher and project manager. (See also the bursar's job profile in the TDA's 'Looking for a Bursar?' publication for numerous other roles and responsibilities the SBM is expected to assume!) Given that scenario, it will not be long before the SBM is overloaded with additional tasks and not able to keep fully up to date with the latest regulations and legal requirements applicable to all businesses and public bodies. In this time of litigation and culpability, a need to provide a safe environment for children and ever increasing expectations from pupils and parents, the role of the SBM is a key one and very much a senior management position with leadership and management responsibilities as well as administrative tasks. The question is therefore raised, 'how does an SBM manage facilities safely and effectively as well as their other responsibilities?' Again, of course, the above argument can be applied to a teaching member of the SBT.

8.4 So, who should be responsible?

Clearly the size and complexity of the school will dictate exactly how the responsibilities for facilities and support services are allocated but it is suggested that for medium-size schools the role of facilities management is formalized and becomes a dedicated full-time post, separate from the school business manager. It is akin to the clearly defined and separate roles of corporate services manager and facilities manager in a commercial organization where corporate services may be responsible for HR, IT, procurement and finance and will also oversee hard and soft support facilities provision.

The private and independent school sector has for many years employed school bursars to perform these support tasks, often linking the role to that of school accountant and clerk to the governors. As the need to attract more pupils and identify new funding streams has developed in both the public and private sectors, the bursar may also take on the roles of business development, marketing manager and fund raiser. These additional roles are now increasingly expected of the SBM as state schools become more integrated into their communities and facilities are required to be open to the public, with spare capacity made available to generate income. The hard fact is that funding has to be chased and pupils attracted to the school as parents/pupils are empowered to select a school of their choice.

8.5 Outsourcing facilities management

Effective facilities management in schools presently relies on a number of specialized departments outside the school advising the school and providing services from a centralized pool. This may, for example, be maintenance support from the local council, school meals provision through a contractor or centralized production unit or grounds maintenance from a contractor selected by the local authority. This provision leaves little control in the hands of the school, yet each of these services is vital to the successful operation of

Table 8.5.1 PFI and PPP

Under these arrangements, private sector money is used to fund the building of a school, then as part of the deal the contractor will operate the school through a mix of hard and soft service providers. In this way the contractor is responsible for providing and maintaining the facilities in an operational state to the local authority for a number of years. The service provision is 'guaranteed' through a range of Service Level Agreements linked to Key Performance Indicators (KPIs). In the event of successful provision, the contractor will be paid their full payment or fee; where a KPI is not fully met there is likely to be a warning process which could lead to a financial penalty. SBMs may well find themselves part of the quality audit process to measure the service outputs and may well also be involved in contract amendments, re-lets and tender evaluations.

the school and any service failing is likely to impact severely on the learning process. Increasingly, with schools controlling more of their budget, there is a drive to gain control of support service provision from within the school, yet the expertise or time to manage these complex functions is not to be found in the existing school business team, nor (given the tasks outlined above) can the SBM do this in isolation.

One option is the outsourcing of the facilities provision through a support services contractor. Currently the most likely outsourced provision will be the school meals service and the daily cleaning of the buildings. However with the advent of the Private Finance Initiative (PFI) and the Public Private Partnership (PPP) schemes (refer to Table 8.5.1), more and more schools are being built and then operated by contractors. More and more SBMs are finding themselves operating in a school managed under such a system and thus supported by a contracts manager or group of managers each responsible for a specific support service provision.

8.6 Best practice: Contracting out

As it is feasible for an SBM to be involved in the process of outsourcing a support service function or range of functions, it is worth describing a very simplified contracting out process. The process that underpins the contracting starts with an output specification or statement of requirement that details what is to be provided by the contractor. This may well have input from the school business team, indeed it should be demanded if the school is to receive the most suitable service provision possible. A number of service providers or contractors will then be invited to develop their solutions for providing services that meet or exceed the outputs specified; these are submitted as 'tenders' and include a price that covers the cost of the service provision and obviously an element of profit. Following tender assessment by a panel of financial and technical experts, again maybe including the school business team, a preferred contractor is selected and arrangements made to assume responsibility for the services. The basis of the service provision is the contract document that is developed based on the output specification and the winning tender submitted. It is signed by all parties, and includes the conditions of contract to formalize the legal relationship. Detailed service level agreements identify exactly what service is to be provided and to what standard, linked to a number of indicators (possibly financial but could also include availability targets, response times, satisfaction scores etc.) that are used to objectively measure the service. A quality audit process will be used to measure these outputs and a management report produced on a regular basis to summarize outputs, issues and activities to the contract management team. When necessary the contract may be formally amended to take account of changing service requirements. (See Table 8.6.1)

Delivering further cost savings and efficiencies will continue to be a driver for schools and central government and the contracted service provision will continue to be seen as an opportunity to deliver such savings and efficiencies. With careful management and a contract that has the scope to innovate and utilize best practice it may be possible for the FM to identify and provide these. Some contracts are written to encourage innovation through a sharing of any cost savings identified between the school, contractor and contract staff, however sometimes costs are driven down purely by selecting the cheapest contract price on initial tender or re-let – this can lead to a degradation in service and longer-term additional costs to rectify a failing contract. The SBM find in this situation that their time managing a failing contract will drag them away from the myriad of other tasks they could be doing.

An effective contract is one that enables the service provider to:

- deliver the services within the price tendered
- deliver to a clearly defined standard
- innovate and share in any efficiencies developed

An in-depth understanding of the business sector in which they are operating and a full appreciation of any stakeholder's expectations will ensure that there is no confusion or concern later down the line. The key person to manage the service delivery will be the FM who is selected to be in daily charge of the contract outputs, ideally (s)he should be based on site, alongside the SBM.

Table 8.6.1 A simplified contracted service provision process

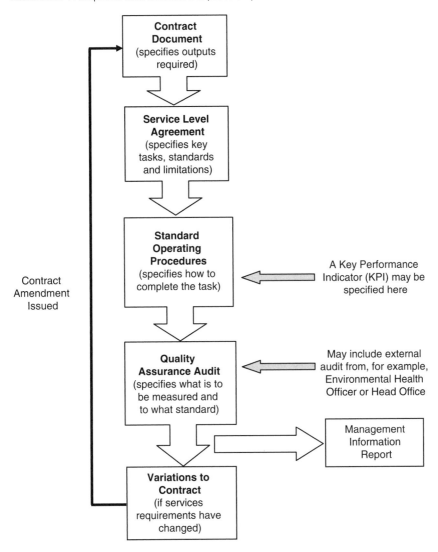

8.7 What can you, as an SBM, expect from the FM?

One of the biggest impacts on the role of the SBM is the interface with facilities management that the 'Building Schools for the Future' programme brings. As schools become learning centres and available to the wider community, a more complex level of facilities management is required. Management of multi-skilled staff operating throughout the year for extended hours each day will be required, facilities will need to be made available and reconfigured to meet varying demands throughout the day and catering, cleaning and security services need to be responsive to differing demands of a wider variety of users of the facilities. Management of this complex facility cannot all be achieved by an SBM and thus the professional facilities manager will play a larger role in supporting the SBM to deliver these requirements. It is not unreasonable to expect the following in terms of professional support:

8.7.1 Effective communication skills

In an outsourced service provision the SBM will have daily contact with the FM – communication is key to ensuring the service provider knows what is expected of them and any changes to the daily routine. In return the SBM will wish to know any issues that are raising and problems that could affect the operation of the school . . . ideally in advance! A best practice exemplar for communication is described in the case study below.

A case study in communication

At the National College for School Leadership, the corporate services manager (SBM equivalent) holds a formal weekly meeting with the FM. Once a month this meeting reviews the monthly management information report and once a quarter this meeting includes the account director from the contractor's head office. Every six months the College Corporate Services Director will also attend the meeting. On a daily basis there is telephone or email communication, or there are face-to-face meetings between contractor and client to ensure that everyone is kept informed of issues and updates. In this manner a strong partnership is built up and the adversarial relationship, which may have been common in the past with outsourced service provision, is avoided.

8.7.2 A clear understanding of client needs

The skill and expertise of the FM will depend on the scope of the contracted out services. It is common to find the FM will either be from a 'hard service' background (engineering, construction, building management) or 'soft services' (catering, cleaning, accommodation services). Whichever background, the FM should have a clear understanding of customer service standards and procedures, they should, for example, understand the expectations of the various stakeholders in the contract (client, student, teacher, parent, local authority etc.) and be able to match these expectations with the provision of the service to the required standard.

8.7.3 Appropriate qualifications

As health and safety is a vital aspect of any service provision, a suitable qualification such as the Institute of Occupational Safety and Health's (IOSH) 'Working Safely' or 'Managing Safely' awards or the National Examination Board in Occupational Safety and Health (NEBOSH) qualifications should be a prerequisite. For food service provision a food safety qualification such as the Royal Institute of Public Health (RIPH) 'Food Hygiene and Safety' Intermediate or Advanced qualification or Royal Society for the Promotion of Health (RSPH) should be achieved by the managers. An FM should be a member of the trade association relevant to their skills and background to demonstrate their commitment to continuing professional development and to be able to access industry research and best practice. For example membership of the British Institute of Facilities Management (BIFM) (www.bifm.org.uk), the Institute of Hospitality (IofH) (www.hcima.org.uk) or of the Local Authority Caterers Association (LACA) (www.laca.co.uk) could be specified in selecting an FM.

8.7.4 Knowledge of financial management concepts and techniques

Financial acumen is a prerequisite for anyone responsible for managing buildings and facilities. Not only is there considerable capital investment in these, and as such they need to be managed in accordance with Treasury procedures, but the repair, maintenance and provision of support services will probably consume over 50 per cent of any school's budget. An FM should be able to not only provide up-to-date budgetary information (income, expenditure and accruals) but also management information showing historical and future trends, budgetary forecasts and statistical analysis. They (or their head office) should also be able to provide costed business cases with options, quotations and 'value for money' recommendations. To assist in this process the school or contractor may provide a Computer Aided Facilities Management software package (CAFM) to manage and record the service provision.

8.7.5 Specialist IT expertise

A key element of the learning facility of the future will be the IT infrastructure that delivers not only the audio-visual aids to teaching, the individual PCs to each learner, but also supports the schools administration, building management, security and possibly community e-learning systems. Again this is a resource that cannot be managed by an 'enthusiastic amateur' but needs establishing, managing, maintaining and repairing by qualified staff. The FM will be responsible for providing a robust yet flexible IT infrastructure to meet the demands now and in the future.

Business Continuity Planning/Disaster Recovery Plan are terms commonly used in business to cover the systems and procedures in place to ensure the organization copes with and recovers from an unforeseen disaster. Schools similarly need risks to be identified and managed and procedures in place to enable swift recovery of vital IT systems, facilities and services – more so when the school sits at the heart of the community's learning and support provision. A facilities manager can manage this risk and ensure that systems and procedures are in place to mitigate against disaster.

8.7.6 Ethical and social awareness

Environmental issues currently dominate the FM press, mirroring the concerns being raised at governmental and community level. Schools are increasingly expected to teach or embed environmental policies within the curriculum and demonstrate their environmental credentials through their buildings and the management of facilities and services. The SBM and FM have a key role in delivering these expectations. Schools should have the skills to manage plant and equipment to demonstrate energy efficiencies and reduce the carbon footprint; the school meal provision should embed healthy eating into the food offers and reduce 'food miles'; waste management should effectively limit and recycle rubbish; building design and refurbishment should take into account environmental best practice, and the daily operation of the facility should embed environmental efficiencies into everything that is provided. All these initiatives will fall to the SBM and FM to manage and deliver to the set targets. There is much information to support managers in implementing environmental procedures; resources such as the Carbon Trust (www.carbontrust.co.uk) and The Chartered Institution of Building Service Engineers (CIBSE) (www.cibse.org) are a good starting point.

8.8 Summary

What is clear is that the role of the school business manager has grown over the last ten years or so to a level where they sit (or should sit) as part of the senior business team and manage a large and vital part of the school's budget and support provision. Their effectiveness in delivering high quality facilities and services can have a direct impact on the success of the learning process and availability of the school to the local community. As the role develops, the SBM will either become the de facto facilities manager or will work alongside an FM provided by an outsourced service provider. It goes without saying that the contract that sets the output standards must be accurate and achievable with clearly defined Service Level Agreements (SLAs). Building and maintaining an effective and trusting working relationship (a partnership) between the SBM and FM is then vital to ensuring the overall success of the school in delivering the educational policies expected and satisfying all stakeholders' expectations.

Further reading

FM World, BIFM's fortnightly journal.

Facilities Management, journal published by MPP Ltd.

Barratt, P. and Brady, D. (2003), '*Facilities Management – Towards Best Practice*. London: Blackwell Publishing.

Reuvid, J. and Hinks, J. (eds) (2001), *Managing Business Support Services*. London: Kogan Page.

Shah, S. (2007), *Sustainable Practice for Facilities Managers*. London: Blackwell Publishing.

Atkin, B. and Brooks, A. (2005), *Total Facilities Management*. London: Blackwell Publishing.

Useful websites

www.bifm.org.uk: British Institute of Facilities Management. Founded in 1993, the Institute provides information, education, training and networking services for over 12,000 members – both individual professionals and organizations. This website will be extremely useful for individuals wishing to develop careers in facilities management or to organizations considering establishing the role of facilities manager.

www.fmassociation.org.uk: Facilities Management Association. This is a website dedicated to the interests of employers providing facilities management services. It provides a useful perspective on current issues in facilities.

The Educational Psychologist

Dr. Jonathan Middleton

9.1 Introduction

School business leaders working with educational psychologists? These are strange sounding bedfellows. One concerned with balance sheets and bank books, the other dealing with some of the most challenged children in our system. Yet if we are to ensure that the UK's expenditure on Special Educational Needs (SEN) is to produce value for money there is surely a case for their worlds to collide, or even come together – especially in the context of 'inclusion' as a guiding principle to our approach to education.

The twenty-first century has seen a shift in policy thinking about provision for SEN pupils. The government's inclusion agenda has placed increased emphasis on educating as many students as possible within mainstream education with a consequent fall in the number of special schools, accompanied by a trend towards co-location of special need provision on the same site as mainstream. Whatever the educational issues, the matter of resources falls firmly into the remit of the School Business Team (SBT).

Education is an emotional business. Everyone cares about the child. Teachers, support staff, multi-agency professionals and parents all rightly claim that promoting the 'best interests of the child' is their motive for action. Nowhere is this better exemplified than in providing for pupils with SEN. The legalities are complex and the proper use of funding designated for SEN by schools and the local authority can be a subject of debate, conflict and frustration. It can also lead to tribunals, emotional stress and wasted resources.

The phrase 'special' is suggestive of something that occurs rarely, or is an isolated phenomenon. As schools know this is far from the case. In 2007 government statistics indicated that nearly 242,600 pupils have statements of SEN across England. That's 2.9 per cent of the nearly 8 million children in school. There are also 1,230,800 pupils with SEN, but without statements, which represents 14.9 per cent of pupils across all schools.

This chapter focuses on the unique role of the educational psychologist and how schools can get the best out of the relationship. It considers the often thorny issues of resource allocation and 'who is responsible for what' that can bedevil relationships without clarity of purpose and trust on all sides. It also considers the current trend for the work of the educational psychologist to shift from providing a traditional school psychology service to a more community focused 'Educational and Child Psychology Service'.

9.2 The legal framework

There are two factors involved in setting the legal context of the work of the educational psychologist.

9.2.1 Qualifications

The provision of an educational psychology service is a statutory requirement upon all local authorities, yet it would come as no great surprise to hear questions from some staff in schools such as: 'Who are these mystery figures?' 'How are they qualified to make critical decisions about our pupils?' 'What is the difference between psychiatry and psychology anyway?' Therefore, if staff in schools are to work productively with their educational psychologist a basic understanding of the role, its parameters and the legal context are essential.

The route to becoming an educational psychologist is clearly defined. A first degree in psychology and a Masters degree (Educational Psychology training) are essential requirements. Educational psychologists must also have at least two years teaching experience and achieved Qualified Teacher Status (QTS). This last criterion is clearly a key element in building relationships, as it's the credibility factor.

9.2.2 The definition of special educational needs

Current legislative requirements for identifying and meeting SEN have their origins in a number of pieces of legislation starting with the 1981 Education Act, but the definition of SEN most commonly used is taken from the Education Act 1996: '*A child has special educational needs if he or she has a learning difficulty which calls for special educational provision to be made for him or her.*' It also says that '*a disability, which prevents or hinders them from making use of education facilities*', amounts to a learning difficulty if it calls for special educational provision to be made.

The Special Educational Needs and Disability Act 2001 provides the statutory framework for the broad 'inclusion agenda' the government has promoted since the turn of the century. This Act established that SEN will be met by mainstream schools unless parents decide otherwise, or that it interferes with the education of other pupils. The Disability Discrimination Act 2001 brought in the requirement that schools must not treat disabled pupils less favourably than others but must also make 'reasonable adjustments' to ensure they are not disadvantaged.

In 2002 a revised SEN code of practice was published. This reflected the experiences of schools and local authorities over the previous decade and provides the detail for the two Acts. The code sets out five key principles which have shaped the work of schools and educational psychologists since then:

- children with SEN should have their needs met
- their needs will normally be met in mainstream schools
- the views of children and parents should be sought and taken into account
- parents have a vital role to play in supporting the education of their child
- children with SEN should be offered full access to a broad, balanced and relevant curriculum in the foundation stage and later years

This was further supplemented in the government publication 'Removing Barriers to Achievement' (DfES/0117, 2004) which emphasized:

- Early intervention – to ensure that children who have difficulties learning receive the help they need as soon as possible and that parents of children with special educational needs and disabilities have access to suitable childcare.
- Removing barriers to learning – by embedding inclusive practice in every school and early years setting.
- Raising expectations and achievement – by developing teachers' skills and strategies for meeting the needs of children with SEN and sharpening the focus on their progress.
- An improved partnership approach – services working together to meet the needs of children and families.

So . . . we have a fully qualified fellow professional who has to work within a regulated framework . . . sounds very similar to the work of other professionals within the school!

9.3 But what do educational psychologists actually do . . .?

Uniquely placed in the system, the role of the educational psychologist is described by one local authority educational advisory service thus:

> We use our skills to help children and young people from 0–19 years who are experiencing difficulties in their development, behaviour or learning in order to promote social inclusion.
> ('A Guide for Parents: Applying psychology to make a difference for your child',
> St Helens MBC)

While the focus of the educational psychologist's attention is the individual child, and some of their work involves engaging directly with individual pupils, much of their work involves giving guidance to teachers on the social and emotional factors affecting teaching and learning. Reports may be written about children for allocation of special educational places, or as part of court proceedings or children's panels.

At present local authorities employ the majority of educational psychologists but in recent years increasing numbers now work as independent or private consultants. It is interesting to speculate if the service may not become a 'commissioned service' at some stage in the future in line with the 'Five Year Strategy for Children and Learners' (DfES, 2004) which describes the Local Authority's role as:

> . . . commissioning and developing new services, such as extended schools and 'educare'; and acting as the champion of parents and pupils, rather than focusing only on direct provision and delivery.

(p. 115)

9.4 Who do they work with?

Well, the key is that they work with 'children', but this definition covers 0–19, so it's best to consider categorizing their work by need. Unfortunately, SEN is an umbrella term covering a huge spectrum of need so it is worth reflecting for a moment on this range:

- Children with learning difficulties, which can be . . .

9.4.1 Moderate (learning difficulties)

Children who have difficulties in areas of their learning and who progress less quickly than other children, and are usually educated in mainstream schools.

9.4.2 Severe (learning difficulties)

Children whose rate of progress is less than half the rate of other children of the same age and may have a statement of special educational need.

9.4.3 Profound and multiple (learning difficulties)

Children with a combination of physical, sensory and intellectual impairment that is very severe. The children are likely to be educated in a special school.

9.4.4 Specific (learning difficulties)

Children who are not making the expected rate of progress in reading, spelling, writing or numeracy.

- Children with hearing impairment, visual impairment, speech and language difficulties, physical disability. These all affect a child's learning and may affect their social development - so these also constitute a 'need'.
- Autistic Spectrum Disorder: Autism is a condition that affects the development of a child's social, communication and imagination skills.
- Attention Deficit Hyperactivity Disorder (ADHD): ADHD is an impairment of activity and attention control. The problem presents as a child who is always on the go, does not settle, has poor concentration, cannot stay still and cannot wait for others.
- Behaviour, Emotional and Social Difficulties (BESD): Behaviour, emotional and social difficulties describes a wide range of difficulties including children who are very withdrawn, children who are hyperactive, children with mental health problems, children who are unable to control their temper and those who are aggressive or disruptive.

Take a break . . . Trend analysis

Check on the number of children of each category of need in your school. Have the proportions changed in the last ten years?

Contact a similar-sized/category school (in another local authority) and 'benchmark' the same indicators.

This activity will give you data to use when calculating resource allocation, value for money and so on. It is valuable management information for decision making. Of course, to make decisions, you have to start with the source of your funds, and the organization which provides them. Or, perhaps more accurately, the person who represents the organization – what is your relationship with that person?

9.5 Managing the relationship

Like any relationship, money issues will inevitably intrude at some point, so let's start there. A key aim of the school business team is to achieve value for money in the use of the school's resources. A key challenge for the educational psychology service is how to use its limited resources to meet the many demands upon it. Perhaps this is the meeting ground for the two. Is there a case for applying 'cold' business concepts, such as the rate of return on investment and cost/benefit analysis to determine how a school should best use the scarce resources available for SEN? Surely, it is worth at least a conversation?

Expenditure on SEN represents a significant proportion of any local authority's budget. The case study below reflects the national context.

St Helens Schools

In 2007/08 (source St Helens Section 52 Budget http://212.248.225.145:8080/publications/Section52Budget07-08version5.pdf) a total of over £3.2 million (out of a budget of approximately £93 million) was devolved directly to schools for SEN and in the case of one large high school this amounted to over £160,000.

St Helens' schools receive funding in four ways:

a) An identified amount in the delegated budget. This amount varies between schools and is determined by a formula based upon a range of socio-economic indicators about the children in the school.

b) School Action funding. This is for pupils on the school's SEN register, who have an Individual Education Plan (IEP) and there is a clear intervention strategy. In St Helens each pupil receives £600.

c) School Action Plus funding. In St Helens, pupils who are involved with other agencies, for example Youth Offending Team (YOT), Social Services, Child Adolescent Mental Health Service (CAMHS) are automatically placed on the School Action Plus register. Initially no additional resources, beyond the normal School Action funding, are allocated. If, however, after two terms the child appears not to be progressing the school may apply for funding to the Provision Agreement Panel (PAP). The PAP is a multi-agency body and meets every three weeks, guaranteeing a much more speedy and flexible response to need than the statementing process. The PAP has the power to recommend up to 30 hours support per week for an individual child which is resourced by the local authority.

d) Statemented pupils. The development of School Action plus provision has meant that the number of pupils in mainstream schools with 'Statements of Special Educational Needs' is declining. In the future these are likely to be few in number and be limited to very complex cases. Additional funding is provided from the local authority.

How a school uses the resources allocated to it for SEN provision is a potential source of disagreement between the school and the educational psychology service. For example, what is legitimate expenditure from the funds provided through the delegated budget? The school may regard it as for 'general' provision for all pupils with SEN, for example, not only contributing to providing smaller teaching groups, teaching assistants and resources but also making a contribution to the general overheads required to run the school. It may or may not be able to provide a clear audit trail demonstrating that funds have been used for their intended purpose. The educational psychologist, on the other hand, will argue that the funding is purely to provide for 'additionality', i.e. to provide SEN pupils with additional resources beyond those the school ordinarily provides for all pupils – thus the school should not use these funds as a contribution to the general running costs of the school.

9.6 A changed context for a changed service

Before proceeding with some suggestions for protocols for managing the relationship it may be useful to consider some recent changes in the nature of the relationship between local authorities and their schools. There are three broad categories of change:

1. The repositioning of the local authority's role from a provider of services to a commissioner of services. It may be argued that the apparent overriding drive from central government to devolve more funding from central local authority services directly to schools could result in schools having to purchase their SEN provision themselves, either through 'buy back' agreements with local authority educational psychology services or from private providers. This is now a well-trodden route for many services previously provided directly by the LA, for example school meals and advisory services.
2. Inextricably linked to the first, is the focus on accountability. In common with local authority school improvement service, the educational psychology service also sees its role as providing 'challenge and support' to schools. Thus while offering 'support' through the services it provides, it will increasingly 'challenge' schools to demonstrate that funds allocated for SEN pupils are spent appropriately and that the school is making the best use of its resources.
3. The movement away from providing support for specific pupils in a school towards 'provision mapping'. In other words, rather than using resources to target one or two Y7 pupils who may exhibit learning and/or behavioural difficulties to provide a course in emotional intelligence for all Y7 pupils.

Bearing these changes in mind, we can now consider some terms of reference ('protocols') to help ensure the work is efficient and effective, *and* satisfies both parties' demands and ethical approaches.

9.7 Protocols

As with so many things in life 'it's good to talk'. In practice it is probably rare for members of school business teams to meet with an educational psychologist and discuss their respective roles and responsibilities as well as to share understandings. The protocols in the box below would not cost a great deal, but if followed could bring about better use of SEN funding. Each of these will now be examined in more detail with suggestions to make the activity work better for both parties.

Example: Key elements of a protocol

1. Set up an initial meeting between the school business team representative and the school's educational psychologist to explore roles and exchange information about the local context.
2. Discuss how the school intends to use the SEN funds allocated through the LA formula.
3. Agree transparent processes for monitoring the allocation of funding designated for SEN.
4. Specify clearly how the funding 'follows' an individual child or group of children. Agree a system for 'tracking' the funding.
5. Agree KPIs so that the school is able to judge value for money (a) in relation to the service it receives from the educational psychology service, and (b) in relation to its expenditure on SEN provision.
6. Agree what the school will provide for the educational psychologist – a room, guaranteed teacher availability etc.
7. Evaluate value for money of provision. This will be linked to clearly demonstrable outcomes related to the development of individual or groups of children. Acknowledge mutual successes and areas for improvement.

9.7.1 Initial meeting

Effective dialogue between any two groups of professionals requires both parties to make serious efforts to understand the other's role and professional culture. The educational psychology service is, perhaps, unique within local authority services. Its direct responsibility is to neither the local authority nor the school, but to the child and his/her parents. Quite rightly, this is a fiercely guarded position – educational psychologists see their role as determining what is appropriate provision, not as securing funding for that provision. They make their judgements independently of any financial constraints that the local authority or schools face. This is not to say that they are 'financially irresponsible', merely that they do not wish to compromise their judgements about the needs of the child because they are also responsible for managing the purse strings.

Schools, of course, have finite resources and have to make choices between the competing demands on them. If the school and the educational psychology service are to work harmoniously, surely there must be merit in an exchange of cultural perspectives as the basis for the establishment of a harmonious working relationship?

9.7.2 Allocating resources

In theory this ought to be straightforward. In 2007/08 St Helens allocated £3,577, 043 for expenditure on special needs (excluding special schools). But what counts as legitimate expenditure on special needs? Expenditure on teaching assistants would seem to clearly fit the bill, as would expenditure on laptops (but will these be exclusively for pupils with SEN?). But what about expenditure on the refurbishment of a workbase – should this come from the general maintenance budget or is it reasonable to fund this from SEN funds? The local authority's scheme of delegation may provide guidance on these matters and can be a useful starting point for discussions between the SBT and the educational psychologist.

9.7.3 Agreeing transparent processes

To expect schools to develop separate accounting regimes so that they can demonstrate they have used the funds designated for SEN as they were intended may be regarded as overly bureaucratic and unreasonable. Equally unreasonable, however, is a scenario in which a school is unable to evidence to the parent of a child who is in receipt of Action Plus funding, how that income has been translated into additional support for the child.

There are concerns in the field that not all is as it should be. The National Association of Special Educational Needs (NASEN), in their submission to the Education and Skills Select Committee on 'Special Educational Needs: separation of assessment of need from funding of provision' (2007:4) (www. nasen.org.uk) makes this point very forcibly:

> Schools need to be accountable for the monies that are delegated to them and there needs to be a more effective system to ensure that those pupils who are being funded to support their special needs are actually receiving that funding.

9.7.4 Determining Key Performance Indicators

Expenditure on SEN in England amounted to £4,477,300,000 in 2006/07 (Hansard, 26/04/2007). Not all of this was spent on educational psychology services, but it is pertinent to ask with this level of expenditure how we know we, the taxpayers, are getting a good return for that investment. At the level of the individual school there is a strong case for agreeing some Key Performance Indicators with the school psychology service. What might these look like?

First KPIs could be agreed in relation to the *consultancy* role provided by the service and as this role is likely to increase in the coming years now may be an opportune moment to investigate how its success or otherwise could be measured. Process indicators would appear to be the most appropriate for this aspect of the role. These could include items such as the 'quality of advice/training given to staff' which might be measured through question-naires designed to elicit how any consultancy provided had impacted upon the teacher's or teaching assistant's classroom practice.

Secondly, KPIs could be agreed in relation to the *intervention* role. While this may be complex the area should not be shied away from. 'Intervention' may be provided by an educational psychologist, or more typically by one of the many 'para-professionals' who now work with teachers supporting individual children. Notwithstanding the complexities of how we demonstrate 'impact' within education – the subject of a book on its own (!) – output indicators would focus on pupil progress measures. These could be based upon academic achievement, behaviour, attendance etc. While the school may not have the time and resources to set up an evaluation framework which would meet the strict guidelines for academic research, they may be able to satisfy themselves that there is sufficient evidence to show that a specific set of intervention strategies for a particular child did have an impact – or more tellingly, did not, and thus represented poor value for money. Once again it may be timely to set up such mechanisms, as the value for money of intensive one-to-one support is challenged.

Value analysis

Try taking any *one* specific activity and . . .

    a) undertake a cost analysis (using the sample pro forma provided here)
    b) estimate 'added value'

Value analysis—cont'd

Now look at the results as . . . (i) a parent; (ii) school.

SUGGESTED PRO FORMA

PROCESS COST SHEET   TERM:

Autumn/Spring/Summer

Details	Process	£
INPUT		
Materials		

Staff costs (wages)
  a) Internal
  b) External		

Expenses (NB: detail)		
Overheads allocation		
TOTAL		
OUTPUT		
Key descriptors		/10

Staff
  a) Number of staff trained
  b) Number of staff given individual advice		

Children
  a) Number of children supported
  b) Behaviour improvement
  c) Number of children experiencing
     SEAL programme
  d) Reduced exclusions
  e) Academic progress (reading age,
     numeracy scores)		

Summary		

9.7.5 Evaluation

This stage flows logically from the previous one. There seems to be much sense in sitting down at the end of the year and trying to evaluate how the service has performed and whether or not the service provision represents value for money. It may seem crudely determinist, but can we put a price on the value of improving a child's behaviour so that she avoids being permanently excluded from school? Some would argue we cannot, yet there are some rough calculations we can make, for example, if the child were to be permanently excluded what would be the cost of finding an alternative place – is this greater or less than the cost of keeping the child in the school?

The activity set out here is not intended as a rigid framework, but a suggestion to stimulate debate over evaluation. You may wish to consider refinements to the process, such as 'weighting' according to different perspectives (the child's, the parents' and so on), but that is a decision for you and your team.

However, a warning note: the benefits to the child may be less easy to quantify. Nevertheless we can use the reports of teachers on the child's self-esteem, relationships with others and the impact the child is having upon other students to provide indicators of the success of any interventions. And if the evidence is that there has been no impact? Surely this is when the school business team should be challenging the appropriateness of the resource allocation, and possibly the quality of the service that has been provided. Whatever happens, it cannot be simply ignored.

9.8 Summary

Educational psychologists and school business managers might appear, at first sight, to be strange bedfellows but there is a strong argument for greater communication between them. Expenditure on children with special educational needs represents a significant proportion of national, local and school spending. If we are to establish that this expenditure represents value for money, mechanisms should be in place to determine the educational outputs from specific resource inputs – this may be challenging in practice, but this should not deter us from making the effort.

References

Alexander, P. A. and Winne, P. H. (2006), *Handbook of Educational Psychology*. New Jersey: Lawrence Erlbaum Associates.

British Psychological Society: www.bps.org.uk.

National Association for Special Educational Needs: www.nasen.org.uk.

Tilstone, C. and Rose, R. (2003), *Strategies to Promote Inclusive Practice*. London: Routledge.

Further reading

Educational Psychologist ISSN: 1532-6985 (electronic journal) 0046-1520 (paper). London: Routledge.

Weare, K. (2004), *Developing the Emotionally Literate School*. London: Paul Chapman Publishing, http://eprints.soton.ac.uk/17608 (accessed 17 June 2008).

Useful websites

www.bps.org.uk: The British Psychological Society website provides an overview of the role and work of psychologists in general, and has a section devoted to the work of educational psychologists.

www.aep.org.uk: Association of Educational Psychologists. The AEP is the independently registered trade union and professional association for educational psychologists. It represents the professional and employment interests of some 93 per cent of qualified educational psychologists working in the United Kingdom, most of whom work for local government.

www.prospects.ac.uk/cms/ShowPage/Home_page/Explore_types_of_jobs/Types_of_Job/ p!eipaL?state=showocc&pageno=1&idno=67: For a brief description of the work of educational psychologists.

The Health Professional
Nick Wrigley

Chapter Outline

10.1 The education context

The role of health workers in a school context has become increasingly complex over recent years. The whole issue of the definition of what constitutes health in the broadest sense has clearly expanded, not least because of the implications of the 'Every Child Matters' (ECM) government initiative. In providing guidance for schools in managing this activity area and the professionals who work within it, it is important to stress at the outset that the senior leaders in a school need to liaise closely with their local primary care trust, social services and the appropriate educational welfare officer of the local authority. In preparing this section of guidance for schools, examples of good practice have been identified. From the case study examples visited and investigated it became apparent that the concept of a 'service level agreement' (see 'legal context') with the education welfare officer or with the school health adviser is not widely practised, and there is no specified allocation of hours to a particular school. However, in all cases, the delivery of an effective service was found to be dependent on the creation of good working relationships with the key professionals who deliver the service (both internally and externally) in a variety of ways. This further underlines the importance of this chapter in providing information and guidance about working with these individuals.

A further complicating factor for many schools has been the policy of closing special schools both in the areas of learning difficulties and behavioural problems. As a result of the policy of 'Inclusion', laudable though it may be, additional pressures related to health issues have been faced by most schools. A structured response to these challenges is essential if the schools are to achieve the desired outcomes of integrating 'special needs' pupils effectively without damaging the educational interests of pupils as a whole. It could obviously be argued that the 'special needs' are not specifically related to health issues, but the greatly increased awareness of school conditions such as ADHD and Asperger's Syndrome mean that many more pupils are considered to be suffering from conditions which educationalists perceive require expert diagnosis and the delivery of relevant treatment.

Current research suggests that as many as five per cent of pupils may suffer from ADHD to a greater or lesser degree and this figure, while it may represent an exaggeration, clearly indicates the level of problem which many schools face.

10.2 The legal context

It is arguable that the health adviser helps the school fulfil the legal obligations of the employer to 'provide a safe and healthy place of work'. Given the legal implications of *in loco parentis*, it is even possible to argue that all (i.e. including students) who are on the school premises regularly, during 'business hours', fall into this category. However, as safety at work is governed by more than 30 Acts of Parliament (with similar legislative boundaries in most countries) and comprehensive general rules backed by codes of practice worked out within specific industrial sectors, then it is probably more sensible to adopt the view that 'health' is a separate, curriculum-based concern.

If this view is adopted, then the health adviser has similar legal status to, for example, a local authority catering provider (indeed, the two activities are linked, as can be seen in this chapter). From this perspective, service level agreements are a natural part of the working terms of reference, and can provide a framework for effective relationships.

In the parent's place

'*In loco parentis*' is a legal phrase explaining the authority of the school and its teachers over their pupils. Literally it means 'in the parent's place'. When you send your child to school, you are surrendering your responsibility as a parent to the school for the duration of school hours.

The courts have held that the school and its teachers must take the same care of their pupils as a careful parent would take of his own children, so parents have the right to expect that the school will protect their children from harm.

To carry out this duty the school is given the same rights as parents while children are in its care. This means, for instance, that a teacher can punish a student (for example, by keeping them in during lunchtime) in cases where a parent might reasonably have done the same thing, even though the parent of that particular child objects strongly to such punishment. A parent's individual preference about discipline is irrelevant when the school is acting in a reasonable manner towards the child.

10.3 The role of the health adviser

To illustrate the complexity and variety of the area of health work which now falls on schools it may be useful to examine the job description provided by one primary care trust in the north-west of England for the job of health adviser. The 'Job Summary' attempts to encapsulate the role by focusing on three general responsibility areas.

The responsibility to:

- 'promote the physical and mental health of the school-age population aimed at enabling them to achieve their educational potential'
- 'empower young people to look after their own health by allowing them to make an informed choice of healthy lifestyles'
- 'deliver a range of health services in multi-disciplinary partnership with children, families and school communities'

The implication is that the health adviser is expected to work as an independent practitioner, unsupervised, within the school, home and community. This places a great emphasis on the commitment and diligence of the individual and the precise nature of that commitment will vary greatly depending on whether the individual is serving a widely scattered rural community or a more concentrated urban population.

The job description then breaks down the specific job in much more detail and it is at this level that the individual school needs to establish (again, by localized agreement as part of the service-led framework) the areas where the skills of the individual professional can best be deployed. Interestingly, it is when schools and health professionals get to this level of detail regarding their operational activities, that the boundaries of the 'three broad responsibility areas' become blurred. This can be seen by looking at how each of these areas is interpreted by both health and education practitioners.

10.4 Promoting general health

The first broad area of responsibility concerns the responsibility to 'promote the physical and mental health of the school-age population aimed at enabling them to achieve their educational potential'. This is interpreted by all of the schools researched as follows: 'the health adviser is expected to employ his/her specialist knowledge and expertise in identifying and prioritizing health care needs of school-aged children within their own designated schools and to independently assess the physical, mental and/or emotional needs of school-aged children within their own caseload'. The health adviser is then asked to 'plan, implement and evaluate programmes or core provision in relation to identified need'.

To deliver this aspect of the service, close collaboration with the school doctor, the psychological service and social services is obviously necessary and it is in this area that the nature of the caseload varies most widely: at the most basic level of assumption, deprived urban settings will have more issues for these professionals to deal with than affluent suburban areas. Maintaining sufficiently regular contact with individuals in respect of this requirement to enable the adviser to monitor the progress of the programme effectively, is clearly difficult in view of the contextual, general responsibilities and caseload which they carry.

Therefore, the conclusion has to be reached that the school and its appointed health adviser need to collaborate in deciding what the priorities should be. It is important that the school discusses the job description with the adviser to achieve this consensus. It is also clear that the priorities may vary according to the nature of the catchment area of the individual school and the background from which its pupils are coming.

Nevertheless, certain areas can be identified as common to all contexts. For example, one area which would be readily identified by the general public is the requirement to initiate and implement individual and whole-school plans for the management of children with diabetes, asthma, epilepsy, allergies or other chronic conditions through multi-disciplinary partnerships. On a day-to-day basis the presence of a sufficient number of qualified first-aiders in the school is a major factor in enabling the school to deliver appropriate support in this area. It is important that staff as a whole in the school are aware of the information regarding such pupils and that they know where to find support quickly in the event of an incident involving such pupils. In the research conducted, concern was expressed by many schools that some parents seem reluctant to reveal necessary information to the school. A further cause for concern in more than one instance was the tendency of some parents to send children to school who were already under the weather and even in some instances reported to the school office immediately on arrival at the school. Where both parents are in full-time employment it was seemingly regarded as acceptable to pass on the problem of dealing with a sick child to the school. The disruption caused to normal working routines for support staff and the danger of spreading infection, quite apart from the inadequacy of proper sick bay provision in many schools, was something most of the schools seemed resigned to, and accepted as inevitable. Further investigation revealed that the 'responsibility' seems to be generally accepted by schools, but it is arguably a matter of wider 'health education' to at least initiate discussions with the stakeholders in the learning community about the extent of responsibility for all parties involved. In the absence of such discussions and agreement, it is not surprising that parents will follow the principle of *in loco parentis*. However, the 'Good Practice' section at the end of this chapter offers a way forward.

10.5 Food, cigarettes and sex

This section relates to the second broad area of responsibility: the health adviser is asked to plan, implement and participate in community-led public health initiatives in response to local need and public policy, both local and national. When examined in detail, it can be seen that the activity again demands cooperation between those involved. Inevitably, responsibility needs to be shared, and this is illustrated by three high profile issues.

The first example of this aspect of the role is the concern nationally about the high level of obesity in the population generally, and of children of school age in particular. Senior staff in schools, and indeed the general public (because of recent publicity involving TV chefs) will be aware of the guidelines provided for school meals provision. Many schools have completely withdrawn the provision of inappropriate dispensing machines even though this may represent a loss of income for the school. The issue of obesity has been given an increasingly high profile over recent years and the collaboration between curriculum-based initiatives and overt school policy in this area is of great importance if the issue is to be tackled effectively.

Another high profile example in which the long-term health of the population can be materially affected by habits adopted at school age is in the matter of smoking. As a public building, all schools now are non-smoking establishments and recent legislation has given this issue a high profile. It is a widely observed conundrum among teachers that parents who smoke tend to be those who are most vociferous in ensuring schools prevent children from doing so! This pressure for action is both local and national and is inevitably a shared responsibility.

The expertise of the school health adviser is also expected in making a contribution to the school's delivery of its Personal, Social and Health Education programme (PHSE) and this incorporates sex and relations education. In the case study schools this was certainly an area where the external dimension was felt to be particularly important and generally effective. Indeed, the job description speaks of providing a 'drop-in service for young people to enable access to health advice and guidance in confidence on all aspects of health, including sexual health'. An element of personal continuity is important here as the health adviser becomes known to the pupils and confidence grows in seeking help and support – but the time demands are extensive if such a personalized service is to be offered . . . with obvious implications concerning resources.

In some schools, the input is formalized in that the health adviser is asked to contribute to and support schools in achieving the National Healthy Schools Standard (NHSS) by ensuring communication with schools and the PHSE coordinator and by attendance at school-based meetings to support this. Later in this chapter we will examine an example of good practice in an individual school to deliver this service.

Every member of a senior business team in every school or learning centre will be aware of the disruption caused by the 'needle days', but it is an area which can be managed well, and it is worth noting that the health adviser is required to promote immunization uptake and individually lead and coordinate on provision of immunization sessions in accordance with Trust guidelines and Department of Health recommendations. The adviser is expected to be competent in, and accountable for, managing emergency situations during school-based immunization sessions including the management of anaphylaxis and delivering basic life support in accordance with the Resuscitation Council UK Guidelines. Part of the responsibility in this area is to ensure that appropriate provision is made for the handling and storage of various vaccines and for the arrangements for immunization sessions. Clearly this cannot be done by the school without professional input and advice, which again emphasizes the partnership aspect of the relationship.

10.6 Home–school relationships

The third, general area of responsibility (to 'deliver a range of health services in multi-disciplinary partnership with children, families and school communities') brings into focus the relationship between home and school. The health professional occupies a unique place in this often fragile framework for action, but it is one which has been found to be crucial for children's development. This is reflected in the change of name in the UK to 'Department for Children, Families and Schools' (DCSF).

One of the major areas of the health professional's responsibility, and one in which the closest cooperation with the school is obviously vital, is to undertake home visits for individual pupils, offering support and continuous assessment with behavioural modification plans and referring to other agencies if necessary. The ability to recognize signs of neglect, sexual, physical and emotional abuse and to take appropriate action according to local and national child protection guidelines represents a very important aspect of the school's role and the specific skill of the health adviser. If indeed every child actually matters, it is all too often the most vulnerable who need the greatest support and those high profile cases which hit the media headlines indicate very often the warning signs were missed. Identifying, assessing and offering additional support to vulnerable children and families (including those at risk of violence and abuse), is an aspect of the school's health responsibility which is very important. Taking part in case conferences and supporting appropriate liaison procedures is an area in which the health adviser can make a major contribution to the well-being of individual children.

At secondary level and especially in rural locations with a large catchment area it is likely that pupils will be drawn from more than one primary care trust and the schools should be aware that detailed practice and specific job descriptions may vary as a consequence. To utilize the skills of individual school health advisers to best advantage, schools have often developed very good working relationships and mutual trust and understanding has grown between the parties. This is certainly an aspect in which both parties need to work consistently in the interests of individual children.

Case study A

The health adviser has a responsibility for a local high school and for several of its feeder primary schools. This has proved to be a particularly beneficial circumstance as the adviser has a good knowledge of potential problem children and families as they progress through to secondary education and is able to give the local secondary school helpful advice on the individual child in question. The record keeping and reporting arrangements made in respect of individual children by the health adviser provide a very useful database for the school as they wrestle with their growing responsibilities under current legislation and the pressure for inclusion for all pupils.

The important point here is that the legitimacy for the arrangement was interpreted by all as being provided by the health adviser's job description, in the section which deals with communication. Here it speaks of 'a requirement to maintain effective liaison and communication with clients and all members of the primary health care team, including educational and other agency staff', and 'advising on the management of common childhood illnesses and complex chronic health issues'. The need to demonstrate 'excellent communication and negotiation skills when dealing with sensitive issues and difficult environments such as child protection concerns, children with special needs, parenting difficulties, mental health and drop-in sessions' is emphasized.

This was interpreted by both parties as the key issue of awareness of all information available – in this case, the teacher's formal and informal knowledge is available to the health adviser.

10.7 Wider responsibilities

There is a fourth, more implicit responsibility which emerged from the research. This involved the sphere of leadership, for, in addition to managing the complexity of their own caseload, the adviser is asked to play a lead role in training and facilitating school staff at a senior level on the management of health issues. More specifically, the common concern expressed by many teachers regarding the disruptive influence which a small number of pupils may have on the class as a whole and the damage this may do to the educational progress of the majority. This brings into focus the issue of the health of the teaching staff. Research indicates that the levels of stress have been of concern to the government and the reallocation of many responsibilities to support staff under national agreements has been an attempt to respond to the challenge. The position and role of support staff and the need to train and develop their skills has been recognized as a specialist role. It is being addressed through the highly successful CSBM and DSBM programmes and increasingly we see such people included in the School Business Team (SBT). The implication for the SBT is clear – clear lines of responsibility and reportage are essential when so many disparate elements of the workforce are involved.

This fourth area of responsibility can be referenced to some aspects of the job description which do not impinge directly on their role within a school, student-focused context, but demonstrate what a complex and demanding role the school health adviser has, and why it has been emphasized that the school and the adviser must develop a close working relationship to maximize the benefit which the individual can bring to the school and its students. It must be noted that their contribution and skills are generally valued by schools, but the 'valuation' differs in individual schools. The involvement of the school business manager seems to be a contributing factor – which is certainly borne out by the responses of teaching and support staff in the case study school situations.

Case study B

The author was invited to attend the weekly meetings of the coordinating group which deals with a range of issues on the general agenda of health and inclusion of pupils. The Inclusion Coordinator is a very experienced teacher who has worked at this particular 11–18 community school for many years and has developed a good working knowledge of the catchment area and the individual and collective problems which the school faces. The weekly meeting has a multi-agency agenda and is attended whenever possible by the Special Educational Needs Coordinator, by the

Case study B—cont'd

Education Welfare Officer whenever available, by the School Health Advisory, by a representative from Connexions and by heads of year if they have specific concerns about individual pupils in their charge which they wish to bring forward for discussion and advice. Local specialist units provide support in areas such as autism and the provision of an eating disorder clinic, and Connexions provide 2½ days a week of support for the school (approximately one day of counselling, one day of mentoring and half a day of anger-management training).

This school also followed the model of case study school A in the fact that the school health advice also served several of the feeder primary schools. This was widely accepted as an advantage and helpful in dealing with transition problems for incoming pupils. The move for some pupils was particularly difficult if they were transferring from one of the very small rural primary schools to a large high school with well over 1,000 pupils.

It was emphasized that the work of this group has grown organically as it has responded to a changing agenda and a range of fresh challenges. What was formally described as the Learning Support Unit has now been redesignated as the Inclusion Resource Centre which can draw on a range of expertise responding to pupil needs. The weekly meeting allocates an appropriate member of the team to respond to a specific case. The objective of being a 'listening school' generates its own problems and these can be exacerbated by the fact that pupils are drawn from three different local authority areas, each of which may follow differing policies in respect of resources and support.

Attending these meetings gave a strong impression of the sense of care in the school and the complex nature of the issues which they face. Self-referral is viewed as a priority among the team who emphasize they are there to listen. Another aspect which struck home forcefully was the fact that many of the matters discussed were multidimensional with some aspects of health but issues of behaviour and attitude involved as well. The closure of special education units for both learning and behavioural difficulties has brought many of these problems into focus and the group agreed that to some extent the weekly inclusion meeting was a bidding process for resources.

10.8 Good practice

At this point we shall return to consider the lessons from good practice in providing a wide-ranging system of support for children through professionals working together.

1. All stakeholders need to be involved
   One practitioner emphasized that her role had changed from hands-on nursing to a role that increasingly involved home visits on behavioural issues and, although

training was provided, this was a difficult area requiring a whole-school policy approach. In turn, this required working closely with a variety of school-staff – some reluctant to recognize each others skills! The school management need to be involved in the health professional's responsibility area of organizing the school to 'promote the physical and mental health of the school-age population aimed at enabling them to achieve their educational potential'.

2. Interpret job descriptions to suit the local context

    This means taking the general, formal (often national) terms of reference and interpreting them within a discrete context – a particular centre of learning. If it is to do this effectively it needs to consider how best it may support its particular set of parents and its specific community. This involves a range of expertise and collaboration between various agencies but surely every child does matter, and ensuring that schools have the ability to rise to that challenge demands imagination and commitment to share the responsibility.

3. Put a 'Service Level Agreement' in place

    Agree the terms of reference for the role reconciling the perceptions of all stakeholders and get these 'signed off' in the form of a 'service level agreement' with an appropriate protocol setting out roles and responsibilities.

4. Set up a communication forum to ensure a similar protocol exists for parents' responsibilities

    The move to 'centres of learning' for whole communities, with school sites containing clinics, social services offices and police/probation centres, is a vision of the future which is fast becoming a reality. The danger is that it can lead to unrealistic expectations concerning the roles of all the professionals involved. A protocol for the processes involved will go a long way to address this issue.

5. One-to-one relationships

    For the senior business team member a general awareness of the issues raised by this chapter is obviously important, but specific areas which require attention in many schools may perhaps be allocated to one person. For example, the lack of proper facilities to deal with children who are ill in school and an awareness of who the qualified first-aiders are, and where they can be contacted if an emergency arises, demand a quality assurance approach based on systems and processes, with one nominated coordinator who can work across academic and administrative boundaries. This set-up encourages one-to-one relationships and has the advantage of ensuring speedy responses, but make sure there are contingency and continuity HR plans!

The introduction to this chapter emphasizes the increasingly complex nature of the school role in maintaining a healthy attitude and lifestyle. Many of the issues which schools are now expected to take an active role in dealing with, are matters which relate to both health and educational policy and every school needs to take a proactive role in supporting its pupils and its staff as a whole internally. Further, it was mentioned at the outset that the policy of inclusion has placed a different series of pressures on schools to create internal policies which enable both the health and education professionals' school to respond effectively to the responsibilities placed on them.

The key message is that 'responsibility' must be accepted by all the stakeholders involved: the health professional may legally be just another service provider, but in this area of activity, the boundaries of service provision impact on every child – who are of course, the responsibility of all the stakeholders involved in the school (see Appendix for the legal position with regard to parents' rights to keep a child away from school). Rather than see this as a burden, a clear set of processes and systems will offer a framework for positive action.

10.9 Summary

The emphasis in the 'Every Child Matters' agenda on 'being healthy' and 'staying safe' has led to an expansion in the role of the school health adviser. The role now covers:

- promoting physical and mental well-being
- providing guidance on healthy lifestyles
- providing health services to children and their families

The role, increasingly, moves beyond the school gates and the health adviser must take a holistic view of families and their health needs.

If schools are to deliver the government's 'inclusion agenda' satisfactorily, it is essential that good mechanisms are established by schools so that they can engage with all those agencies concerned with the well-being of the child.

Further reading

Medical Officers of Schools Association (2006), *Handbook of School Health* (18th edn). Stoke on Trent: Trentham Books.

Rogers, E., Moon, A. M., Mullee, M. A., Speller, V. M. and Roderick, P. J. (1998), 'Developing the "health-promoting school" – a national survey of healthy schools awards', *Public Health*, 112, (1), 37–40.

Useful websites

http://www.schoolhealthadvisor.co.uk/: This website contains useful material for schools to download for use in PHSE lessons.

http://www.healthyschools.gov.uk: This website is a general website established to support the government's drive to improve the health and well-being of young people. It has many useful links.

Appendix

Medical reasons for keeping a child away from school

When the medical officer can override a parent's wishes and insist on absence

Regulations about exclusion from school on health grounds are made by the area specialist in community medicine (child health). Even if your family

Table 10.9 Guidance on infection control in schools and nurseries

	Recommended period to be kept away from school (once child is well)
Rashes and skin	
Athletes foot	None
Chickenpox	For five days from onset of rash
Cold sores (herpes simpex virus)	None
German measles (rubella)	Five days from onset of rash
Hand, foot and mouth disease	None
Impetigo	Until lesions are crusted or healed
Measles	Five days from onset of rash
Molluscum contagiosum	None
Ringworm (tinea)	None
Roseola	None
Scabies	Until treated
Scarlet fever	Five days from commencing antibiotics
Slapped cheek of fifth disease(parvovirus)	None
Warts and verrucae	None
Diarrhoea and vomiting illness	
Diarrhoea and/or vomiting (with or without a specified diagnosis)	Until diarrhoea and vomiting has settled (neither for the previous 24 hours)
E.coli and haemolytic uraemic syndrome	Depends on the type of E.coli seek FURTHER ADVICE from the CCDC

Continued

Table 10.9—Continued

	Recommended period to be kept away from school (once child is well)
Giardiasis	Until diarrhoea and vomiting has settled (neither for the previous 24 hours)
Salmonella	Until diarrhoea and vomiting has settled (neither for the previous 24 hours)
Shigella (bacillary dysentery)	Until diarrhoea and vomiting has settled (neither for the previous 24 hours)
Respiratory	
'Flu' (influenza)	None
Tuberculosis	CCDC will advise on action
Whooping cough (pertussis)	Five days from commencing antibiotic treatment
Others	
Conjunctivitis	None
Glandular fever (infectious mononucleosis)	None
Head lice (nits)	None
Hepatitis A	There is no justification for exclusion of well older children with good hygiene who will have been much more infectious prior to the diagnosis. Exclusion is justified for five days from the onset of jaundice or stools going pale for the under fives or where hygiene is poor.
Meningococcal meningitis/septicaemia	The CCDC will give specific advice on any action needed
Meningitis not due to meningococcal infection	None
Mumps	Five days from onset of swollen glands
Threadworms	None
Tonsillitis	None
HIV/AIDS	HIV is not infectious through casual contact. There have been no recorded cases of spread within a school or nursery.
Hepatitis B and C	Although more infectious than HIV, hepatitis B and C have only rarely spread within a school setting. Universal precautions will minimize any possible danger of spread of both hepatitis B and C.

Source: Health Protection Agency, 2007 (www.hpa.org.uk)

doctor thinks a child is fit to attend, the school can exclude him if the medical officer – not the headteacher – issues a notice that the child is to be excluded on health grounds. The child will not be allowed back until the medical officer gives permission.

Local Authorities

Ron Lofkin

11

11.1 Introduction

The concept of the middle tier of delivery in the English education system has been adopted in many countries of the world – South Africa, the USA and most European countries have a 'local authority', literally, an 'authority' which dealt with 'education' on a local basis. These organizations have controlled education delivery since at least 1903 in, for example, the USA. In England, the phrase has been formalized to the extent that it is an established label (until recently, called the local authority – LA) with connotations and implications of bureaucracy. Therefore, although focusing on a UK context, the arguments and principles set out here have international validity.

For the last two decades successive government reforms have led commentators to pronounce that this middle tier approach (the local authority) was about to wither – and with good reason. The introduction of Local

Management of Schools (LMS) in the 1990s, and David Miliband's initiative, the 'New Relationship with Schools', heralded a shift from local authorities being a provider of services to becoming a commissioner. The English experiment of providing direct funding of schools from central government is being studied closely on an international basis. The involvement of private companies in education is another feature, with transfer from local authority control of the management of education services in areas such as Leeds and Bradford clear examples of the practice. The opportunities for schools to distance themselves from the local authority by becoming self-governing trusts or City Academies merely add weight to the arguments of those prophets of their demise. All these policy initiatives, and others, may be seen as evidence of the diminished role of the local authority in the provision of education.

And yet, they are still with us and can often count school leaders among their staunchest allies! How do we resolve this conundrum – after all, aren't the reforms intended to 'liberate' schools from local authority interference? In this chapter, we will argue that local authorities have maintained effective working relationships with schools because of their capacity for adaptation and because they meet defined needs – particularly as education becomes increasingly discrete and individualized, and these needs become more disparate and localized.

11.2 Legal framework

Local authorities are generally charged with responsibility for *the welfare and education of every child* in their local area, although this responsibility may vary from country to country. However, *in all countries*, local authorities operate within a statutory legal framework. This may differ in terms of the extent of devolved responsibility, but generally, all may be regarded as having three broad functions:

1. To provide democratic accountability for the education service to the local population.
2. To strategically manage education and young people's services.
3. To commission services which maximize efficiency and effectiveness of local education delivery.

How does this framework translate into practice? Well, there is a variety of different reportage systems (refer to function 1 above) but local politicians usually figure in the equation, and regular 'reports' from officials are also a feature. With regard to function 2, this usually includes:

- Special Educational Needs (SEN)
- planning the supply of school places
- making sure every child has access to a suitable school place, or has suitable provision made for them
- supporting and challenging schools, and intervening where a school is failing its pupils

With regard to function 3 – 'commissioning services', this translates into:

- allocating funding to schools
- (specifically in the UK) implementing the refurbishment or rebuilding of every secondary school over the next 10 to 15 years through the 'Building Schools for the Future' initiative
- maximizing delegation of both funding and responsibility to schools, to help them become more genuinely self-managing, and able to make well-informed choices among different service providers

In the UK, the most recent redefinition of the role of LAs was announced at the Local Government Association's Social Services Conference in 2004 when the then Secretary of State set out the direction he envisaged for LAs. The main elements were:

I. The steady transition of the local authority from *provider* of services to a *commissioner.*
II. The authority being a strategic community leader and *champion* of pupils and parents – the driving force behind children's trusts.
III. The need to make a distinction between national services locally delivered and services for which *local prioritization* is best.
IV. Authorities as *empowerers and supporters* for front-line agencies (schools, children's centres etc.) and ensuring delivery of those national services.

(Teachernet-www.teachernet.gov.uk)

Given the worldwide interest in this model, and considering the strategic context, this definition (or more accurately, these terms of reference) will be adopted in this chapter.

11.3 The relationship in practice

While all local authorities have a number of statutory responsibilities they must meet, at the heart of the relationship between the LA and its schools is school improvement. The emphasis now placed on the local authority's responsibility to provide 'challenge and support' to its schools is juxtaposed with the development of the role of what is entitled (in the UK) the School Improvement Partner (SIP). In the USA, the SBO often acts in this capacity. This person is employed and managed by the local authority yet is also a 'partner' of the school. This development has forced a significant realignment in the relationship between local authorities and their schools. We have established that the local authority is responsible for monitoring educational standards within its locality, and indeed, is required to intervene should a school be causing concern. However, the SIP, who may or may not be a permanent employee of the LA, is the person who challenges the school on its standards and pupil outcomes. How is this apparent anomaly resolved? One local authority in the UK devised its own model in response to these developments (refer to case study A, below).

Case study A: A new relationship

In the case of Stockport MBC the approach taken has been to maintain the role of what was formerly known as the link adviser (who formerly would have carried out the functions now allocated to the SIP) but to reposition it to meet the new context.

A key driver in the development of the 'New Relationship with Schools' is the desire to reduce the bureaucratic burden on schools brought about by the need to provide separate reports on its performance to a range of stakeholders. The solution, to replace the separate reporting requirements with a 'single conversation' with the SIP, places the SIP 'centre stage' with the local authority possibly on the sidelines. Stockport LA, keen to ensure this did not happen, and with the support of its headteachers, developed a strategy which they believe combines the benefits of the SIP role with that of a link adviser by carefully delineating the two roles in remodelling their approach to providing a school improvement service to schools.

Under the new model the integrity of the 'single conversation' is maintained as each headteacher or senior leadership team now meets with the SIP and LA link adviser *together*, although the 'single conversation' is actually a series of

> ### Case study A: A new relationship—cont'd
>
> conversations held throughout the year. At these meetings the SIP focuses on standards and pupil outcomes, while the link adviser ensures that there is a response by the local authority to issues raised by the SIP. During the year the SIP and link adviser are in contact with each other – the link adviser providing the SIP with contextual information on the school as a result of visits and conversations. A concern in Stockport was that at most the SIP would spend only three days per annum in the school, whereas link advisers spend from 3–12 days per annum in each school, according to individual need.

11.4 The relationship in reality

So, how does this 'new relationship' between the local authority and its schools play out in practice? The school improvement service focuses its initial attention on the information provided in the SIP's Note of Visit for each school. In other countries, this data is similarly generated, but may come from different sources and from different methodologies (for example, annual monitoring data). From its analysis of this data the local authority is able to determine where best to target its interventions. Increasingly the approach is to focus on specific strategic areas, which if improved, are likely to provide most leverage for overall school improvement. Thus the focus could be on management (for example, the leadership provided by middle leaders), or pedagogy (for example, the teaching of thinking skills). Next come the 'challenge' and 'support' functions in ensuring these strategic improvements take place.

The 'challenge' focuses not on the school's performance, but rather on what the school needs to do about its performance. This represents a shift in emphasis in keeping with modern management approaches wherein delegation of responsibility is wrapped up with the motivational concept of 'ownership'. As John Adair pointed out:

> Fashions change in organizational thinking . . . At one time, centralization of decision-making was all the rage. Now decentralization is the order of the day, and this applies as much, if not more so, to the public sector as to the private. Once the heads have received (your organizational) blessing on their set of objectives they must be free to carry them out without interference from you. If

they come to you for support you must give it to them. They are the ones who are going to make things happen, not you.

(John Adair, 2005)

Local authorities have generally followed this advice and determined that for sustained improvement the most successful approach is likely to be to get the school to take ownership of the 'Plan of Support'. The role of the link adviser is therefore to work with the school to achieve this understanding – in essence to bring the school business team to a position where it is they who are requesting the deployment of the School Improvement service's resources. Once agreement on an improvement plan has been secured the role switches to that of support – refer to Adair! This will clearly be determined by the particular needs of each individual school, but includes activities such as leadership training and development, financial training, subject reviews involving all aspects of a department's work, project planning, observation of lessons focused on specific themes, for example provision for gifted and talented pupils, and so on.

Take a break . . . The pros and cons of working together

Take a few moments to reflect on the Stockport model. Is this 'mix' likely to produce a better cake or is it a recipe for confusion? It may be useful to consider the pros and cons of each role separately before considering the benefits/drawbacks of the two working in tandem. I've set out some below to start you off . . .!

Role	Positive features	Negative features
SIP	External to school	Doesn't have an in-depth knowledge of the environment
Link adviser	Familiar with school	
Link adviser + SIP working in tandem	Bring both external and internal perspectives	

11.5 Monitoring and evaluation

Demonstrating the effectiveness of school improvement activities is complex. At any one time an individual school may have instituted a whole raft of initiatives intended to improve student outcomes. When so many variables are altering, how does the school determine the relative impact of each particular input on its changed outputs? And in the case of the local authority's school improvement service, how do schools identify and quantify the benefits of the relationship?

The difficulty is that much of what the school improvement service does may be regarded as largely 'enabling' in character. First, by helping the school to focus its attention, determine its priorities etc. Secondly, by providing support to schools to put in place key building blocks, such as effective leadership and appropriately structured curricula. Further, the service is not free – in Stockport (refer to the case study) a large school will pay approximately £15,000 per annum under a Service Level Agreement (SLA), with smaller schools paying in the region of £8,000 p.a. It is worth noting that this does not equate to a fixed number of days per school. There is an understanding among Stockport headteachers that resources will be targeted according to need and that if a school has a specific issue to deal with it will receive more of the school improvement service's resources. So how is value for money demonstrated in this area?

International comparisons are difficult in that the 'opt out' decision is not available in most other countries: it is compulsory to use the LA services. However, in the UK, the choice *can* be made to opt out of LA services if the school feels they can get a better deal elsewhere. Many LAs have lost 'critical mass' in terms of provision of services, and the LA has then had to close down such services. Interestingly, no school has ever opted out of the service in Stockport and sought to source its school improvement support from elsewhere. This may be regarded as a broad indicator that the local schools see the service as providing value for money. Similarly if, overall, the local authority is meeting its pupil progress targets this, too, might be regarded as an indicator of the effectiveness of the service. More direct indicators include: feedback from Notes of Visits; formal meetings with headteachers who are usually fairly quick to say if a particular intervention has been helpful or not (!); and feedback from staff who have been engaged in developmental activities. However, these are suggestions – the fact is that measuring the impact and effectiveness of School Improvement services may be problematic.

The relationship between the local authority and its schools will, potentially, require further reassessment globally as central governments continue with policies of encouraging diversity of provision.

Take a break . . . Cost/benefit evaluation

In the table below is a list of indicators a school might wish to use when evaluating the benefits and impact of the local authority's school improvement service. For each indicator, what might be the key positive phrases/signs and key negative signs? Again, I've started you off . . .

Indicator	Typical words/activities	
	Positive	Negative
Feedback from curriculum leaders on the impact on teaching and learning	Curriculum leaders request repeat visits by the team. Annual review meeting.	
Feedback from curriculum leaders on impact on leadership and management		
Improvement in school's quality assurance processes		
School more confident in delivering 'stay safe' agenda		
School more confident in delivering 'be healthy' agenda		
Support in delivering 'make a positive contribution' agenda		
School more confident in delivering 'achieve economic well-being' agenda		
School more confident in helping school to raise academic achievement of pupils		
Challenge to SBT's strategic thinking		
School believes it has an enhanced capacity to improve		
Positive Ofsted judgements		
Self-evaluation processes are rigorous		

11.5.1 Enabling

In particular, the opportunity to gain Trust status raises interesting questions. If a more arm's length relationship were to develop between Trust schools and their local authority, would this result in further movements away from local authority-commissioned services towards schools sourcing them themselves? At present this may appear unlikely as it would require significant investment by a private company in order to be able to provide a similar service. However, as private companies increasingly penetrate the education sector, to such an extent that Leeds and Bradford local authorities' education services, for example, are now provided by private companies, such a scenario ought not to be discounted. Increasingly, therefore, it will be important for local authorities to demonstrate the vitality of the relationship and the positive benefits to be had. Case study B below illustrates how such vitality can be enabled.

Case study B

Shortly after the appointment of a new headteacher a local school was inspected by Ofsted. The school's standards had been declining over a number of years and it was not a huge surprise when the school was given a Notice to Improve. The school improvement service team met with the school's senior leadership team with the aim of getting them to acknowledge the issues they faced, and to take ownership of the solutions. This was a positive process. The school improvement service was welcomed into the school and a package of support agreed. The package included:

- the introduction of a Quality Assurance system
- a focus on key subject areas which needed to improve
- LA consultants working with middle leaders, and at subject level
- LA advisers working with the SLT on whole-school issues in order to provide direction

These strategic initiatives were translated into Action Plans, key objectives were established, and mechanisms for regular feedback put into place. Thus a robust partnership was established with the school. Respective roles and responsibilities were clearly defined – most crucial of which was that the *responsibility for school improvement lies firmly with the school*. The local authority's role was to work with the school to develop its internal capacity. If the school succeeded, it would be because *their project* was successful, not because of an externally imposed agenda.

Pleasingly, the school successfully had its Notice to Improve removed at the first attempt and standards at Key Stage 4 have shown a significant improvement. The school now has quality assurance processes described as 'second to none' and has developed its pupil tracking systems to a sophisticated level and is now able to predict with great accuracy pupil outcomes. Overall, staff morale is significantly higher and staff have developed a much clearer understanding of their role in delivering the 'standards debate'. Crucially, pupil attitudes towards school are judged by the local authority to be much better.

11.5.2 Key principles of the relationship

This case study demonstrates how, through the establishment of an effective relationship, a powerful force for school improvement can be generated. So what are the key principles that underpin how the relationship works best?

1. Absolute clarity about roles. The school is responsible for school improvement. The local authority's role is to challenge and support the school in its efforts to bring about improvement. If the school succeeds it will be because of its own actions, if it fails it is similarly responsible.
2. Mutuality. This may seem paradoxical in the light of the previous statement, but it is essential that the partners regard each other as 'on the same side', albeit with different roles. Here, it's about recognizing the 'added value' each brings to the role.
3. Honesty of feedback. School improvement is a challenging area. There may be difficult conversations to be had, but the relationship will not flourish without a willingness to look openly and honestly at what is working and what is not.
4. Engagement with the whole team. If the school improvement service is to be used to maximum advantage by the school, it is important that the whole of the senior leadership team (in both organizations) is engaged from the beginning. An early meeting with the SLT, possibly spread over an afternoon, or even an extended residential, can be an effective method for establishing the common purpose needed to work together successfully.
5. Documentation where appropriate. For example, the Note of Visit is a key document for the agreed recording of evaluative judgements about the school, its priorities for action and key responsibilities. The Note of Visit needs to be completed accurately and checked carefully.

Five key principles in the relationship

1. absolute clarity about roles
2. mutuality
3. honesty
4. engagement with the whole team
5. documentation

11.6 Future challenges

As service delivery within local authorities moves from the old LA model to provision through children and young people's services and the government continues with its diversity agenda future changes are inevitable. We consider two possible areas for further thinking:

1. the shift to multi-agency provision
2. the move towards more targeted services

1. While school improvement remains a key strategic aim, the pre-eminence of agendas such as 'Every Child Matters' (ECM) in the UK and 'No Child left Behind' in the USA, as overarching policy frameworks, has brought significant challenges to both the local authority and schools. Bringing together previously separate delivery arms, such as social services and education to deliver a coherent, integrated service focused on the ECM agenda is complex. These services have very different cultural perspectives, traditions and priorities. To generate effective synergy between them will require significant shifts in the cultures of all involved. There are concerns among some school leaders that the core educative purpose of schooling, as they perceive it, will be marginalized within this broader agenda. Local authorities will need to demonstrate this is not the case – the possibility that schools might opt for Trust status if they fail to do so is a very real one.

2. A second challenge may come from changes to the way resources are devolved to schools as, increasingly, local authorities shift the balance between universal and targeted provision towards more emphasis upon targeted support. In Stockport a key challenge is how to close the gap between learners, and its approach to intervention is to focus the resources it controls on identified groups of pupils, for example pupils who are at risk of not making two levels of progress during a particular Key Stage. In targeting its resources, the local authority does of course run the risk of alienating its 'successful schools' because they will receive less of these resources. There is a potential double whammy here – if the 'successful schools' are successful with less local authority support they may take the view that they don't need the local authority! Thus the school improvement service could, conceivably, start to be viewed as having a largely deficit role. This would be a concern. Nothing could be further from its intentions. There is a strong desire to work with all schools on their individual agendas.

These are only two of the possible changes and shifting scenarios . . . as a member of the school business team, it would be sensible to perhaps begin to engage in such debate about 'futures working' with the local authority representative. If you do this, then at least any change that does occur won't come as a surprise!

11.7 Summary

The role of local authorities in the provision of education services to their local communities continues to shift with the political tides. Local authorities still have key statutory functions to fulfil. Increasingly, local authorities are becoming commissioners, rather than providers, of services but they still have an important role to play in challenging and supporting their schools to raise standards of achievement. The advent of the SIP, coupled with the government's 'New Relationship with Schools', has caused a realignment of the relationship. Schools will want value for money from their local authority school improvement advisers, and local authorities will wish to ensure their schools are doing their best for their children. Relationships built on the following principles and practices are likely to prove fruitful and in the best interests of all parties:

- absolute clarity about roles
- mutuality
- honesty
- engagement with the whole team
- documentation to support action

Further reading

Adair, J. (2005), *The British Journal of Administrative Management*. London: Institute of Administrative Management.

Halsey, K., Judkins, M., Atkinson, M. and Rudd, P. (2005), *New Relationship with Schools: Evaluation of Trial Local Authorities and Schools* (DfES research report 689). London: DfES.

Department for Children, Schools and Families (2008), *Role of the School Improvement Partner*. London: DCSF. Also available at: www.ncsl.org.uk/media/13C/F7/sips-brief-edition-3.pdf (accessed 14 August 2008).

Ward, H. (2007), *The Educational System of England and Wales and its Recent History*. Hastings, UK: Ward Press.

Useful websites

www.dfes.gov.uk/localauthorities/index.cfm: Website managed by DCSF to provide information for local authorities on a wide range of issues. Useful for determining respective roles of central and local government.

www.lga.gov.uk/sponsibilities: Website of the Local Government Association (LGA), used to promote the views of local authorities on a wide range of topics.

The Sports (wo)man
Graham Lewis

Chapter Outline

12.1 Introduction

The 'Every Child Matters' (ECM) agenda in the UK has its equivalents in other countries: for example, the USA has a similar programme entitled 'No Child Left Behind', and South Africa launched its own programme in 2008. In all cases the introduction of these programmes has led to educational institutions having to address, *as equally important*, areas of activity which previously may have been regarded as marginal – sport can be regarded as such an activity. The guidance and focus is overt: help children 'be healthy' is the UK imperative, and in the USA it is equally emphasized, with federal funds and philanthropic foundations set up to help tackle obesity. In the UK, the introduction of specialist 'schools' has formalized this development, with schools focusing on enterprize, ICT, the arts and sports as specialisms of equal status. It is, however, worth noting that the USA has long done this informally, with sport 'scholarships' a common feature of the educational context.

In the UK, there is a further imperative in the link to the requirement of all schools to provide a 'core offer' of services through the extended schools agenda and the obvious connection to after-school activities.

In any event, educational institutions have sometimes responded by 'bringing in' expertise – on a fee-paying or voluntary basis. This makes sense when one considers that the staffing base of most institutions – especially primary schools – is unlikely to contain a specialist in any one sport, or indeed, in exercise in general. This chapter focuses on getting the best out of the resource and the relationships by asking the professionals:

- what they think could enhance their input
- about examples of good practice they have seen
- what schools should expect from them
- what they expect from schools!

12.2 The legal context

Anyone visiting a school is there by permission of the headteacher, who can withdraw that permission at any time, merely by asking that person to leave. (S)he is then trespassing and the police may be called to remove her/him. This is clear enough in terms of parents, for example, but the situation is complicated by the delivery of 'services'. For the sake of brevity and clarity, it will be assumed here that there is no difference between services provided without charge and services paid for by the school – although, it is stressed, there are subtle differences between the two contexts, and these should be checked with the relevant legal advisers.

In practice, anyone who offers services to an organization (the 'provider') has a duty to provide them with reasonable care and skill. A 'reasonable' standard is that shown by ordinary, competent people in the same field. If the recipient of the service (the 'client') suffers financially or is harmed in any other way by negligent or incompetent services, the provider can be sued for damages. Dissatisfied clients can often get help from professional associations, which try to uphold standards among their members – but this is an area of activity which is so new that there is little case study precedent. Most organizations and reputable individual coaches have professional indemnity (PI) insurance, but invoking this is a lengthy and often unsatisfactory process. The most practical approach is probably to simply check the professional status of the individual or organization (for example, qualifications), be assured about PI and ensure there is clarity, in writing, about the nature of the service. This last point is the starting point for good practice (see below).

12.3 Good practice

The first step is to ensure that any claims about the nature or quality of the service are set out in writing. This is because the provider may not legally make a false claim under the Trade Description Act 1968 – either knowingly or recklessly. This should be done in a positive manner, using something like the pro forma (see below) which X school has devised for such events.

Once the terms of reference are received, then it is good practice to invite the provider into the school to discuss the elements which then make up the contract.

Case study: School A

WITHOUT PREJUDICE

Dear . . . . ,

Thank you for your note/further to our conversation regarding basketball coaching, I am delighted that you are able to provide this service for X school.

As part of our quality assurance processes, we would ask you to complete the attached pro forma. This will help set up terms of reference for the session(s), which we can then confirm at a preliminary meeting between [yourself/your representative] and an authorized representative of the school, to be arranged within three working days from receipt of the pro forma. Once the terms of reference have been agreed, we will then issue a contract which will formalize the service.

If you have any queries, please do not hesitate to contact . . .

PRO FORMA

Feb. 2007 – Q.A.Serv.v.3 Doc

Information Regarding [Basketball Coaching]

1. Initial Contact Details

'Flier'	Telephone/email	Other
Date:	Date:	Date:

⇨

Case study: School A—cont'd

2. Name of Supplier

3. Contact Details

4. Details of Service

5. Personnel Involved [with Qualifications]

6. Professional Indemnity Details

7. Other Information

8. Preferred/Possible Dates/Times for Preliminary Meeting

REVERSE

School A: Quality Assurance Process for Services Procurement

1. Initial contact details are recorded on QA.Serv.Doc

2. QA.Serv.Doc. sent to provider for preliminary information.

3. Meeting of both parties within three working days of receipt of completed Q.A.Serv.Doc. to agree terms of reference for contract.

4. Contract to be issued by school within two working days

⇨

Case study: School A—cont'd

5. Completed copy (signed) to be received *prior* to service delivery.

6. Evaluation and feedback to be issued to provider within ten working days of completion of service provision.

12.3.1 The halo effect

This procedure may appear cumbersome, but it sets the tone for the meeting, which becomes a discussion between two professionals of equal status. This is important in sport-related services because of the 'halo effect' which every teacher is aware of. This is the effect noted by Asch in 1946, and other psychologists since then, that reputation and personal charisma will skew perceptions: the total impression formed by an individual is unduly influenced by one outstanding trait or achievement. In effect, some people are favoured simply because of who they are (their background, demeanour, 'track record' etc.), and even if their actions are not in keeping with their reputation, others will excuse them. In an educational context, it is something which every teacher is trained to recognize in both themselves and others, so that every child is treated equally. The phenomenon is actually more evident in the worlds of commerce and industry, where such training has not occurred. We see this frequently at Everton, when leading industrialists, political figures and even academics meet Premier League footballers, and become 'star-struck'. It is generally true to say that teachers and other education-based staff are a little more 'grounded' – particularly in primary schools where the breadth of sport played is greater, and therefore (say) football (or 'soccer' as I know it!) is not as powerful an influence.

Nevertheless, given the high profile of sport internationally, schools and senior staff are not immune to the effect. This is why we actually prefer the procedure adopted by schools such as in the case study above. It shows that the institution is focused on the service, and not the provider. As Rachel Brown, the Everton and England goalkeeper notes: 'I am a qualified teacher who happens to have a role which is tangential to "mainstream education", but is no less valid for that. I am as interested in the outcomes of the session as much as the teacher is.'

12.3.2 The meeting

This brings me to the second element of good practice: the meeting should have an agenda, which is based on the terms of reference, and we have found that in many ways it follows the format of a lesson plan – with the outcomes as the prime focus. These can then be formalized as Key Performance Indicators (KPIs) for the contract. While we have encountered some common KPIs (such as, 'all children involved in the session') and can suggest these, we prefer to start with a clean sheet. This is simply because we regard each school as a discrete institution, and it will therefore have its own priorities.

We have some strong views about who should attend the meeting, as we have found that the most successful and sustainable events are those where the preparation and commitment is evident. From our experience, the headteacher should *not* be the prime point of contact or coordinator/driver. Their involvement should be at the beginning and the end of the interaction. Having written the letter, it is only good manners that dictate that the headteacher should at least greet the provider (or representative) and open the meeting. In terms of the meeting itself, the administrator (or increasingly, the school business manager – SBM) and the nominated teacher (attending the session) should represent the school. This latter point is important: although professionally qualified, we believe that the principle of *in loco parentis* still applies while the child is in school. As a service provider, we cannot have this delegated to us without every individual child's parents' or guardians' written permission. Schools have found it more cost-effective (administrative savings) to have a nominated member of the teaching staff present at the session, and it can also result in savings in terms of PPA 'cover'. It is perfectly legal and acceptable to use the event to release teaching staff for non-contact time.

The teaching member of staff has the greatest input at the initial meeting, particularly in terms of setting and agreeing outcomes, but beyond this, the main point of contact should be the administrator/SBM. We have found that this arrangement minimizes the demands on academic staff and also enhances communication in that most of the queries and issues revolve around logistics of timing, equipment and so on. This arrangement also works well in ensuring a whole-school and community approach, as the administrator/SBM is usually the focal point for ensuring all staff, parents and other stakeholders (for example, bus companies) are aware of the weekly/monthly schedule of events, and of any implications (for example, late opening, limited admission for parents etc.) which may impact. In addition, the SBM is well placed to explore other opportunities from the relationship (refer to the case study, School B, below).

Case study: School B

This small primary school (130 pupils) had strong links with the local basketball team, which ran regular coaching sessions at the school. By using their name and expertise to support an application for Sports Council Funding, they were successful in securing several thousand pounds to purchase equipment and employ specialist contractors to devise and put in place playground markings. This raised the profile of physical activity during playtimes, and reinforced the coaching sessions.

12.4 Preparation

At Everton, we regard the event as an educational experience, and therefore this demands preparation. We are conscious of the demands of the National Curriculum, and recognize that although there is a move towards enjoyment and a possible consequent relaxation of the intensely tight timetable schedules, the event is still a granted privilege for us – even more so when we are paid! In the good practice we have encountered, this preparation is discrete to the school and its context, and is obviously therefore devised and agreed at the initial meeting. Again, there are, however, some key general points, such as the requirement for the session(s) to complement Key Stage objectives, and the link to ongoing programmes of daily physical activity.

Apart from these educational elements, the biggest issue is that of equipment and venue. Although schools have undertaken a risk analysis and have a risks register, it is unrealistic to expect schools to have 'state-of-the-art' equipment for all sports. Schools must ensure that providers recognize this and it will inevitably be a major issue for some – particularly in ensuring that, for example, every child participates – if the provider supplies the equipment. Ideally, the meeting and the preparation will address and minimize the problem through organization, professional expertise and experience. At Everton, we have addressed this issue through the 'Healthy Schools Bus' initiative (see below) which illustrates good practice.

Case study: The Healthy Schools Bus (HSB)

Everton Football Club, Liverpool City Council Children's Services and Arriva transport work in partnership on the HSB project.

Preparation takes place months in advance of the visit of the HSB to primary schools in Liverpool due to the intensity of the schedule of visits. The HSB is generally at a school at 8.30 a.m, stays all day until after school and is at a different school each day of the school term. Consequently the HSB engages over 145 primary schools, 8,000 children and 500 teachers and teaching assistants throughout the school year. Initial research of schools equipment in a random number of schools helped us make the decision for the HSB to be totally self-sufficient, storing all the equipment we needed on-board the bus.

The Process
There are three stages:

1. Pre-visit
This was mainly done by Pat Grace, HSB coordinator at Liverpool City Council. Schools were sent letters providing information about the concept of the HSB project and an invitation to coordinate the date of their visit. Visits were ordered geographically (north Liverpool, central Liverpool, etc.) but each school was asked to select a date from a selection of three dates. The bus firstly went to schools in north Liverpool School Sports Partnership then central, south-central then south.

The schools are asked to send out consent forms to obtain the Year 3 children's height and weight during the HSB visit. Schools are made aware of the dimensions of the bus and are asked to provide an appropriate place to park which must be within 50 metres of an electrical power point to plug the HSB into. Schools also provide information on how many classes and children there are in the year group – usually two classes per year group, per school, each with approximately 30 children. Each class has two one-hour sessions, with one class before lunch and one after. Letters are sent to headteachers who pass on the information to the Year 3 teachers to inform the children regarding PE kit. The school organizes the sports facility, playground or hall, which, weather dependent, is at our discretion.

Risk assessments are written with regard to accessing and being on the HSB, and school risk assessments are carried out for the sports facility. Schools are asked to provide two members of staff (teacher and/or TA) per class.

2. The Visit
On our arrival at the school we brief the Year 3 teacher. This includes splitting the class into two groups (usually 12–15 per group), start time, children wearing PE kits, correct footwear etc. and we always go to get the class from the classroom so the group doesn't arrive before we are completely ready.

Case study: The Healthy Schools Bus (HSB)—cont'd

The curriculum has been devised from the National Curriculum using PE/science units of work relevant to the age of the group. Differentiation and extension activities are always provided. Copies of the lesson plans both for the physical activity and the healthy lifestyle lessons are given to the teachers in a file along with extension activities and other information at the end of the visit. Teachers are asked to hand out HSB diaries and pedometers and are given instructions, after school, on how the children are to use them.

3. After the Event

School Sports Partnerships provide School Sports Coordinators who at each of their primary schools arrange a convenient time to visit the children between two to three weeks after the visit of the HSB. For 20 minutes or so they provide a brief recap of the HSB lesson contents and also review the HSB diaries the children have been given.

The HSB has visited a good number of special needs schools including schools for the blind, hearing impaired schools, schools with severely mentally and physically disabled children, emotional and behavioural difficulty schools and schools for children with autism. For these schools the HSB teachers undertook at least one pre-visit where we would learn about specific requirements for the children. On the day, the core lesson content remained the same but the delivery of it was specifically designed to meet the needs of the school. Often we used a combination of our PE equipment with some of the school's specialist equipment, providing stringent plans and structures for the school day. These visits seemed to be the most rewarding of all, both for ourselves and the whole school . . . health is after all, an issue tailor-made for inclusion!

12.5 The event

At last, the day of the event dawns: from the provider's perspective there are only two expectations or concerns: the biggest worry is that of parking. When Everton use the Healthy Schools Bus, we have already 'scoped' the premises, and have agreed with the administrator/SBM the space, student 'flow', spectator area and so on. However, if the provider is an individual with equipment, then it is important that this is protected: they are not being precious – it is their livelihood! Further, if it's heavy, then the closer to the activity area the better as you don't want them injured prior to the event.

The only other expectation that concerns the provider at this stage is that of delivering the service, so a quick greeting from the administrator/SBM, followed by some time and space, with some water, is all that is required.

It is at this point that the school is entitled to expect the best from the provider. This involves the professional expertise the school has asked for, and the approach should reflect the expectations. A full knowledge of practical educational issues in delivering the service – both general and specific – is a minimum requirement. For example, an awareness of the general principles of behaviour management, coupled with specific knowledge of the school's particular discipline/behavioural code is a minimum that we at Everton insist upon. This will of course, have been agreed at the meeting, and is part of the preparation process by the provider.

Surprisingly, this is as much as needs to be said about the event: we would simply expect schools to 'trust the process', as the provider has had to.

12.6 The review

There are two elements to the review: the follow-up and the corrective action.

The follow-up should be an integral part of the service delivery (refer to the Healthy Schools Bus case study) and if the outcomes have been previously agreed in the terms of reference, then this part of the process will simply take care of itself. The key issue here is that the follow-up *should take place*. We have experienced a tendency in clients to see the event as the main part of the delivery process, with the follow-up as an anticlimax. It is interesting to note, in conversations with other, more generic training and management development providers, that this is a common occurrence – particularly if the event itself has been a valuable experience. However, as professionals who value the educational outcomes, we at Everton perceive the service to be in *two equal parts*; and in the follow-up, we believe that the teacher should 'lead'. In the follow-up stage, our role is to support the teacher – it is the focus on 'what has been learned' which gives the value to the school, and the provider should never forget that.

With regard to 'corrective action', it would be foolish to say that things *always* go smoothly, so if there is a 'non-conformance' (in the agreed delivery process), most providers and clients will want to review the event. The key issue here is that this part of the review should be a constructive meeting, rather than 'a blame session'. Establishing this culture is firmly in the school's control if for no other reason than the fact that the provider wants a long-term relationship, and obviously there is a reputational risk! What providers want is an objective assessment of added value and a dispassionate review of how the non-conformance can be avoided in the future. It is a part of the quality process which most professional organizations subscribe to, and they will accept that the proposed improvement may not be enough for clients to retain their services. The objective is to ensure it doesn't happen again.

Arguably, this is exactly what schools also want, but we have found that there is a tendency among schools to subjectivity. This is understandable, given the focus on students who are currently under their care, and this is why we stress that the terms of reference are so important. If they are strong, then the review is more objective and, dare we say it . . . businesslike! The difference in perspectives is partly contextual: service providers in the field of sport and education take a longer-term view as this is the future of a new area of activity. The issues of obesity and health are government priorities, and sport is seen as a preventative measure. Service providers see longer-term benefits such as, in Everton's case, a larger future fan base, and yes, at least a financially neutral position for the activity. Schools necessarily view this element of 'Every Child Matters' as one of a number of competing priorities, and, it has to be said, have greater pressures regarding the academic achievement of their current charges . . . Ofsted still rules! The aim of this chapter is to help schools get the best out of the professionals who can help them achieve both priorities.

12.7 Summary

Summary of key points to ensure good practice:

1. good documentation is not bureaucracy
2. a formal meeting agenda helps establish the ground rules
3. agree KPIs as part of the terms of reference
4. ensure a nominated point of contact
5. stress good communication for the benefit of the whole school
6. preparation is the key
7. equipment: just make sure everybody knows the limitations
8. let the professionals do their job
9. corrective action is constructive
10. be creative in getting maximum use of the event

References

Asch, S. E. (1946), 'Forming impressions of personality', *Journal of Abnormal and Social Psychology*, 41, 258–90.

Further reading

Epstein, J. L. (1995), 'School/family/community partnerships: Caring for the children we share', *Phi Delta Kappan,* 76, 701–12.

Useful websites

www.evertonfc.com/community/healthy-schools-bus.html: This site provides comprehensive information about the Healthy Schools Bus programme.

www.sportengland.org: Sport England's role is to 'Create an active nation through sport'; it is a non-departmental public body and National Lottery distributor, committed to creating a world leading community sports development system and increasing participation in sport.

www.youthsporttrust.org/page/home-welcome/index.html: The Youth Sport Trust is a registered charity, established in 1994. Its mission is to 'build a brighter future for young people by enhancing the quality of their physical education (PE) and sporting opportunities'.

13 The Transport Professional
Mat Chapman

13.1 Introduction and legal context

Local authorities must provide free transport for children to and from school if they live more than walking distance away. For children under 8, the distance is two miles, and for children aged 8+, it is three miles. The distance is that which is 'the shortest possible route' – regardless of the danger to children on that route.

The result of this sort of ruling is the number of cases almost gleefully reported by the media: you know the sort of reportage . . . an example is provided in the box below. There are a number of options available to the local authority to help it meet some of the objections, for example discretion to help if the child is deemed 'needy'. However, this is fraught with social tensions, as some parents refuse such assistance on the grounds of perceived stigmatization. This phenomenon is well known to schools regarding free school meals, where some parents refuse to claim them on the grounds that it is a 'hand-out' and they don't want to be *seen* to be needing it.

Example: Next door to safety

Figure 13.1 Wayne Round lives just round the corner from Daniel.

Wayne has to walk to school because he lives just inside the 2-mile limit, while Daniel's house is just over two miles from their school. So while Daniel sits safely on the bus, Wayne has to cross several busy roads as he makes his way to school because his mum has to pay . . . and with three other children at school, she can't afford the fares.

Steve Jones from Borcestshire local authority said: 'We have spoken to Mrs. Round, and have offered to help, but we have to draw the boundaries somewhere!'

How this transport is provided is relatively straightforward: The LA or school can:

- issue passes for use on public transport (including trains)
- run its own bus service
- employ other vehicles such as taxis

Each of these methods has its own particular problems, some of which will be more familiar to senior managers in schools than others – depending on the type of school. For example, independent private sector schools have extensive experience of running their own bus service, and are aware of the sensitivities surrounding safety of the bus itself, whereas in the state sector, the concern may revolve around the route or safety 'on board'. Both sectors are also conscious of the 'reputational risk' concerning behaviour on public transport.

It is perhaps one activity area which local authorities may be delighted to pass on to federations or large centres of learning when these two structures become more commonplace, but in the interim the key element of the legal context is that local authorities are responsible for the safety of children travelling on their school buses, or waiting for them at school. They can be sued for negligence if a child is hurt because of inadequate supervision.

With regard to other transport situations such as trips, it is worth noting that there are no national regulations about school trips. However, local authorities make their own regulations which cover such things as insurance and ratio of adults to children etc. In this case, the matter of transport is certainly in the hands of the educational institution organizing the trip. The Royal Society for the Prevention of Accidents (RoSPA) provides comprehensive guidance on roles and responsibilities (www.rospa.com/safetyeducation/schooltrips/part1.htm).

13.2 Legal responsibilities

Before undertaking any school trip you are legally required to carry out a written risk assessment. Schools have a duty of care towards pupils and in an activity where there is an element of risk, you will need to show that you have considered, and as a result taken, 'all reasonable precautions'. As part of your legal health and safety duties, your school will need to show that there is effective communication at all levels.

13.2.1 Local authority

- is responsible for the negligence of any teacher which arises in the course of their employment
- is under a duty to determine policies for the school curriculum
- should state which school trips need governors' consent, for example overnight stays

- should provide guidelines for procedures on school trips, including staff/pupil ratio
- should offer advice on insurance

13.2.2 Governors

- are responsible for the general conduct of the school
- can modify LA policy for the school curriculum, including extracurricular activities
- need to be sure that a school trip has a clear educational value
- must ensure that arrangements are in accordance with LA guidelines and regulations
- must ensure that the school can run efficiently in the absence of anyone on the trip

13.2.3 Headteacher

- is responsible for seeing that the LA and governors' policy is implemented (in accordance with their own conditions of employment)
- has a responsibility to ensure that all school trips comply with LA and school regulations in every respect; and if this responsibility is delegated, it must be to a 'competent' person
- must ensure that activities are properly planned and supervised and that the pupils' safety is paramount

13.2.4 Teachers

- have a common law duty to act as a 'reasonable parent'
- must ensure the meticulous planning and preparation of the school trip including a risk assessment of all activities
- are responsible for all pupils in their care throughout the entire trip
- must safeguard the health and safety of pupils both on the school premises and in authorized activities elsewhere
- must maintain good order and discipline at all times

13.2.5 Non-teachers

- must accept the normal common law duty of care to act as a 'responsible parent' towards the children
- are not held as accountable as teachers

The RoSPA website is a valuable resource and a visit is highly recommended.

The implications of this legal context and other issues will be addressed in this chapter, but the emphasis will be on how to make each situation safer in the most effective and efficient manner by using the expertise of the professionals who work in this sector. For example, transport managers are required to have extensive training before taking up their positions, and anyone who has taken a Public Service Vehicle (PSV) driver's test will tell you it's not a straightforward task! More significantly perhaps, their experience is worth 'tapping into' – there's not much they haven't seen, and in my experience are happy to help!

Oh by the way, there's one common legal situation concerning money! Take a look at the case study below.

I've forgotten my bus money, mister . . .

Two of the children getting on to the bus have forgotten their money; which one of the following will the driver do?

    a) refuse to let the children on the bus; make them make alternative arrangements to get home
    b) talk to a teacher so that (s)he can confirm their travel
    c) let the children travel and sort out the payment later
    d) ring the garage asking the manager for advice

I know it's not widely known, and if it is, it could be regarded as a recipe for unscrupulous parents, but answer c) – 'let the children travel, and sort out the payment later'– is correct. The legal position is that you don't refuse travel to a minor, even if they don't have the fare. For me, this is a clear 'driver' (sorry for the awful pun!) for ensuring the two professions get together and sort out a 'code of conduct'. More of this code later, but if linked to 'good citizenship' as part of the 'Every Child Matters' agenda (ECM), then both parties (driver and children) will benefit.

13.3 Trains and boats and planes . . . and buses

The emphasis in this chapter will be on buses, as these are the vehicles of mass transit which most closely interact with the majority of educational institutions. In other words, they actually come to the school, and usually have to enter the premises, or intrude on its surrounding infrastructure and community (the streets around the school). It is, however, worth noting that there is an increasing rigour about enforcing rules governing general behaviour on trains, with several high profile cases concerning 'feet on seat' incidents by students. In effect, this means there is a higher 'reputational risk' involved, and therefore the same high standards should be applied to both bus and train behaviour, thus minimizing the risk of a 'two-tier' approach, and consequent mixed messages to students. Other than remote areas of Scotland, I can't think of too many educational institutions regularly using boats and planes – but the same rules regarding higher reputational risk apply . . . the less common, the more high profile the incident!

Behaviour policies are a fixed feature of schools, as education seeks to instil sustainable, society-friendly habits and attitudes into children. However, there is a natural and understandable reluctance to extend these 'into the streets' – even if only because of concern that, *by implication*, a legal obligation will be laid upon the school.

Unfortunately, in a 'business' where reputation counts for a lot in terms of marketing (for students), schools need to consider the risks vs advantages of extending a policy into (at least) this situation. The critical point is that the journey home (whether walking or on transport) is the last event of the day where *the school*, rather than a number of individuals who belong to the school, is evident. There is a critical mass which dissipates gradually as the children reach their homes or as they are 'distributed' by the transport to their separate destinations – and this 'critical mass', by association, 'belongs' to the school. The perception – unfair though it is – counts for more than the reality, and parents are the ones who hear stories in the community and read the papers.

So much for the 'stick' in terms of extending the policy into the streets, there's also a 'carrot'. The idea behind a behaviour policy is the enhancement of a culture for learning, and in the USA, using the 'transport event' as such a tool is a more common phenomenon. The case study below illustrates the point.

Case study: Learning while travelling . . .

Margaret Ellen Kalamanowicz, supervisor of transportation and food service at Kent County Public School, Chestertown, Maryland, was recognized for a Pinnacle of Achievement award at the ASBO conference in October 2006 for her work in tackling behaviour on school buses. As she noted . . . 'although the term "learning

Case study: Learning while travelling . . .—cont'd

environment" evokes the image of a classroom, we all know that education also takes place in many other settings; even a school bus can be a place to learn!'

During an in-service workshop for drivers in her district, attendees saw the need to encourage better bus-riding habits among elementary school students. This goal is now being realized through the Character Counts Bus Ridership Recognition Program. To promote good riding habits, drivers regularly complete a form that identifies well-behaved students who are recognized by their principal and invited to an ice cream party sponsored by Lions Club. After one year, elementary schools in the program had reduced bus discipline referrals by 60 per cent. In addition, the feeder middle school is experiencing fewer incidents.

13.4 Too 'American' will never work here? Why not?

Anyway, rationale given, point made (I hope), let's now look at how the relationship between the bus company and the school can be enhanced. Let's start with the management: at the First Group, we operate as a collection of semi-autonomous divisions, so the regional senior management team have a certain amount of devolved power. On the other hand, most of the rules and regulations surrounding school transport are fixed, so there's not much flexibility in terms of 'adjustment' to Standard Operating Procedures (SOPs). Nevertheless, with the introduction of the First School Bus Company – like Yellow Buses in the USA – it is recognized that education is a 'special case', so it's worth inviting a representative from management into school to have a general discussion about your particular school.

This is because we recognize that all schools are different, and even if you don't have school buses calling at your school, we know that children will use buses at some time and that the responsibility for ensuring appropriate behaviour is a general, societal one which devolves on both organizations. As an example of this, most bus companies are now aware of the legal obligations placed upon schools to ensure (at least) safer recruitment of staff. The First Group takes this very seriously indeed, and all managers are aware of their responsibilities in this area of activity. Indeed, the company is working across the group to ensure raised awareness is a feature of the group's recruitment practices. Working with Manchester Metropolitan University

two programmes have been designed – one focused on the roles and responsibilities of drivers, the other on those of managers. They've done this because
they know that such awareness is in itself a feature of enhanced safety, and
will be delighted to discuss this with the school. From the school perspective,
surely any senior management team in any school would want to know that
their efforts to ensure a 'safer culture' in their school is being mirrored by the
organization which precedes/takes over from them at the beginning and end
of the day?

13.5 Operational improvements

Anyway, moving on from this occasional relationship, let's now focus on a
more pragmatic and operational area of activity and the relationship between
the two practitioners – the driver and the teacher/HLTA/ SMT representative.
To put this in context, take a look at the following box.

Case study

A driver drives up to the bus stop near, or at, the school, hoping to load the children
on to the bus; the children are pushing and running about while he is driving to the
stop. What should he do?

a) stop the vehicle and wait for things to calm down and don't open the doors
   until everyone is standing still
b) ring the garage for help
c) call a teacher over to help
d) refuse to let the children on, turn the vehicle round, and take it back to the
   garage
e) report the problems that he has had to his manager the next day, so that the
   manager can record the problems and take them up with the school

---

Actually, this is cheating a bit, because the *current answer* is a), but it's
not ideal. It presupposes a level of expertise in terms of behaviour management which, let's face it, even many teachers struggle to acquire. There are
also the added complications of the driver's own upbringing, experiences and
values with regard to 'discipline' and what (s)he perceives to be 'appropriate
behaviour' – bearing in mind the inevitable age difference between even the
youngest driver and the children. When you add to the 'mix' the particular

policy of the school with regard to its behaviour policy, it can be seen that the issue needs a discrete analysis. It demands a level of critical thinking which requires training and development common to both organizations. In this scenario, without knowing the unique terms of reference which is produced by the interaction of these factors, there really isn't much of an option for the driver.

I would also argue that, in view of the current litigious culture of society, the driver is protecting both the school and the company, in that (s)he is taking responsibility and undertaking an ad hoc risk analysis. However, it wouldn't be unreasonable to expect some sort of dialogue to discuss issues such as these with staff – in advance. Indeed, at First Group, we would be delighted to actually visit with a bus and talk over these potential issues with both the children and the staff – but perhaps more importantly, given the 'safe' element of ECM, it could be an opportunity to embed some of the work in the curriculum.

13.6 Summary

I think the key message here is that an alliance between the school and the company is actually not just desirable, but in practice, essential. Neither can do without the other, but the 'shotgun marriage' can be made to work. There's one final case study which I think illustrates the point better than any constructed argument. Take a look at the box below.

Case study: For whom the bell tolls . . .

The school bus has left the school and is starting to drop the children off at different stops; every time the driver gets near a bus stop the children keep ringing the bell over and over again. As a driver, what would you do?

a) stop the bus until they stop ringing the bell
b) carry on so that you can get the children off as quickly as you can; explain the situation to your manager so that (s)he can make the school aware
c) ring the garage explaining the situation
d) take the children back to the school
e) talk to the manager when you get back to the school
f) ensure that the vehicle has a restriction of one ring on the bell mechanism, restricting the number of times the bell rings

The answers *are* b) and f). Now, having asked this question of many education professionals, most people are unaware that there is such a thing as a 'one ring mechanism'! If for no other reason than learning of the existence of such a thing, a discussion in advance would have helped here. Similarly, there's a lack of knowledge about what the school can do.

The First Group take these issues seriously, and many of these scenarios are incorporated within our training manuals. However, they would be much enhanced if education professionals engaged with us to take into account particular, discrete circumstances . . . professional to professional.

Useful websites

www.firstgroup.com/YSB/index.html: Yellow School Bus Commission. This site is useful for those interested in the issues involved in home to school transport.

www.rospa.com: The Royal Society for the Prevention of Accidents – the website provides valuable information on the statutory rights and responsibilities of all parties involved with the transportation of young people and provides guidelines on good practice.

www.teachingexpertise.com/articles/school-transport-part1-basic-law-and-best-practice-1347: A useful site which outlines both the legal position with regard to home–school transport, as well as addressing practical considerations, such as safety.

Glossary of Abbreviations

ABH	Actual Bodily Harm
ACPO	Association of Chief Police Officers
ADHD	Attention Deficit Hyperactivity Disorder
BATNEEC	Best Available Technique Not Entailing Excessive Cost
BESD	Behaviour, Emotional and Social Difficulties
C&S	Consequences and Sequel
CAFM	Computer Aided Facilities Management
CAMHS	Child Adolescent Mental Health Service
CfA	Council for Administration
CIBSE	Chartered Institution of Building Service Engineers
CoRT	Cognitive Research Trust
CPD	Continued Professional Development
CQI	Continuous Quality Improvement
CSBM	Certificate of School Business Management
DATT	Direct Attention Thinking Tools
DCSF	Department for Children, Schools and Families
DfES	Department for Education and Skills
DSBM	Diploma of School Business Management
DTI	Department of Trade and Industry
ECM	Every Child Matters
EI	Emotional Intelligence
FE	Further Education
FMSiS	Financial Management Standard in Schools
HLTA	Higher Level Teaching Assistant
HRM	Human Resource Management
HSB	Healthy Schools Bus
I of H	Institute of Hospitality
IAM	Institute of Administrative Management

IEP	Individual Education Plan
IOSH	Institute of Occupational Safety and Health
KPI	Key Performance Indicators
LACA	Local Authority Caterers Association
LEA	Local Educational Authority
LMS	Local Management of Schools
LPSH	Leadership Programme for Serving Heads
LSA	Learning Support Assistant
MMU	Manchester Metropolitan University
MOU	Memorandum of Understanding
NASEN	National Association of Special Educational Needs
NCSL	National College for School Leadership
NEBOSH	National Examination Board in Occupational Safety and Health
NHSS	National Healthy Schools Standard
OPV	Other People's Views
PAP	Provision Agreement Panel
PFI	Private Finance Initiative
PI insurance	Personal Indemnity insurance
PMI	Plus points, Minus points and Interesting points
PPA	Planning, Preparation and Assessment
PPP	Public Private Partnership
QTS	Qualified Teacher Status
RAISE online	Reporting and Analysis for Improvement through Self Evaluation (online)
RIPH	Royal Institute of Public Health
RoSPA	Royal Society for the Prevention of Accidents
RSPH	Royal Society for the Promotion of Health
SBO	School Beat Officer
SBT	School Business Team
SDP	School Development Plan
SEN	Special Educational Needs
SENCO	Special Education Needs Coordinator
SIP	School Improvement Partner
SLA	Service Level Agreement
SLT	Senior Leadership Team

SMEs	Small and Medium Sized Enterprizes
SOPs	Standard Operating Procedures
SSP	Safer Schools Partnerships
SWOT analysis	Strengths Weaknesses Opportunities Threats
TA	Teaching Assistant
YOT	Youth Offending Team

Index